Fresh Ways
with Pork

Time-Life Books Inc.
is a wholly owned subsidiary of
TIME INCORPORATED

FOUNDER: Henry R. Luce 1898-1967

Editor-in-Chief: Jason McManus
Chairman and Chief Executive Officer: J. Richard Munro
President and Chief Operating Officer: N. J. Nicholas, Jr.
Editorial Director: Ray Cave
Executive Vice President, Books: Kelso F. Sutton
Vice President, Books: George Artandi

COVER
A roasted pork loin is sliced to reveal its stuffing of spinach, mushrooms, and chestnuts. This dish combines the stuffing from the recipe on page 52 with the instructions for preparing and cooking a boned pork loin in the recipe on page 50. The accompanying gravy is made from wine and stock stirred into the juices in the roasting pan.

TIME-LIFE BOOKS INC.

EDITOR: George Constable
Executive Editor: Ellen Phillips
Director of Design: Louis Klein
Director of Editorial Resources: Phyllis K. Wise
Editorial Board: Russell B. Adams, Jr., Dale M. Brown, Roberta Conlan, Thomas H. Flaherty, Lee Hassig, Donia Ann Steele, Rosalind Stubenberg, Henry Woodhead
Director of Photography and Research: John Conrad Weiser
Assistant Director of Editorial Resources: Elise Ritter Gibson

EUROPEAN EDITOR: Kit van Tulleken
Assistant European Editor: Gillian Moore
Design Director: Ed Skyner
Chief of Research: Vanessa Kramer
Chief Sub-Editor: Ilse Gray

PRESIDENT: Christopher T. Linen
Chief Operating Officer: John M. Fahey, Jr.
Senior Vice Presidents: Robert M. DeSena, James L. Mercer, Paul R. Stewart
Vice Presidents: Stephen L. Bair, Ralph J. Cuomo, Neal Goff, Stephen L. Goldstein, Juanita T. James, Hallett Johnson III, Carol Kaplan, Susan J. Maruyama, Robert H. Smith, Joseph J. Ward
Director of Production Services: Robert J. Passantino

HEALTHY HOME COOKING

SERIES DIRECTOR: Jackie Matthews
Picture Editor: Mark Karras
Studio Stylist: Liz Hodgson
Editorial Assistant: Eugénie Romer

Editorial Staff for *Fresh Ways with Pork:*
Editor: Charles Boyle
Researcher: Sebastian Thomas
Designer: Paul Reeves
Sub-Editor: Wendy Gibbons
Studio Assistant: Rita Walters

Editorial Production
Chief: Maureen Kelly
For the series:
Assistant: Samantha Hill
Editorial Department: Theresa John, Debra Lelliott

U.S. Edition:
Assistant Editor: Barbara Fairchild Quarmby
Copy Coordinator: Colette Stockum
Picture Coordinator: Betty H. Weatherley

Editorial Operations
Copy Chief: Diane Ullius
Production: Celia Beattie
Library: Louise D. Forstall

Correspondents: Elizabeth Kraemer-Singh (Bonn); Maria Vincenza Aloisi (Paris); Ann Natanson (Rome).

THE COOKS

The recipes in this book were prepared for photographing by Pat Alburey, Jacki Baxter, Allyson Birch, Nicola Diggins, Antony Kwok, Dolly Meers, Lyn Rutherford, and Michelle Thompson.

THE NUTRITION CONSULTANT

PATRICIA JUDD trained as a dietician and worked in hospital nutrition before returning to college to earn her M.Sc. and Ph.D. degrees. She has since lectured in Nutrition and Dietetics at London University.

Nutritional analyses for *Fresh Ways with Pork* were derived from McCance and Widdowson's *The Composition of Food* by A. A. Paul and D. A. T. Southgate, and other current data.

Library of Congress Cataloging in Publication Data
Fresh ways with pork.
(Healthy home cooking)
Includes index.
1. Cookery (Pork) I. Time-Life Books. II. Series.
TX749.5.P67F74 1988   641.6'64   88-8582
ISBN 0-8094-6033-5
ISBN 0-8094-6034-3 (lib. bdg.)

For information on and a full description of any Time-Life Books series, please call 1-800-621-7026 or write:
Reader Information
Time-Life Customer Service
P.O. Box C-32068
Richmond, Virginia 23261-2068

Time-Life Books Inc. offers a wide range of fine recordings, including a Rock 'n' Roll Era series. For subscription information, call 1-800-621-7026 or write Time-Life Music, P.O. Box C-32068, Richmond, Virginia 23261-2068.

THE CONTRIBUTORS

JOANNA BLYTHMAN is an amateur cook and recipe writer who owns a specialty food shop in Edinburgh, Scotland. She contributes articles on cooking to a number of newspapers and periodicals.

SILVIJA DAVIDSON studied at Leith's School of Food and Wine in London and specializes in the development of recipes from Latvia, as well as other international cuisines.

JEREMY ROUND, a former deputy editor of the *Good Food Guide*, is food correspondent for *The Independent* in London and the author of a book on Turkish regional cooking.

BARBARA SAUSE is an Arlington, Virginia, food writer and consultant who received a Grand Diplôme from École de Cuisine La Varenne in Paris; she has written articles for *Cook's* and *Cooking Light* magazines, and has contributed to other volumes of Healthy Home Cooking.

HILARY WALDEN is a food technologist. She has written numerous books and articles on all aspects of cooking. She has also developed and tested new products for major food companies and has presented cooking demonstrations for British television.

The following people also have contributed recipes to this volume: Maddalena Bonino, Jo Chalmers, Caroline Conran, Antony Kwok, Norma MacMillan, Cecilia Norman, Emma Ogden, Lyn Rutherford, Louise Steele, Sebastian Thomas, and Jeni Wright.

Other Publications:

THE TIME-LIFE GARDENER'S GUIDE
MYSTERIES OF THE UNKNOWN
TIME FRAME
FIX IT YOURSELF
FITNESS, HEALTH & NUTRITION
SUCCESSFUL PARENTING
UNDERSTANDING COMPUTERS
LIBRARY OF NATIONS
THE ENCHANTED WORLD
THE KODAK LIBRARY OF CREATIVE PHOTOGRAPHY
GREAT MEALS IN MINUTES
THE CIVIL WAR
PLANET EARTH
COLLECTOR'S LIBRARY OF THE CIVIL WAR
THE EPIC OF FLIGHT
THE GOOD COOK
WORLD WAR II
HOME REPAIR AND IMPROVEMENT
THE OLD WEST

This volume is one of a series of illustrated cookbooks that emphasize the preparation of healthful dishes for today's weight-conscious, nutrition-minded eaters.

Fresh Ways with Pork

BY

THE EDITORS OF TIME-LIFE BOOKS

TIME-LIFE BOOKS / ALEXANDRIA, VIRGINIA

Contents

Pork Char-Shiu

Vinegar Pork with Garlic

Light Gumbo

Pork and Spinach Terrine

3 Dishes with an Unusual Twist 98

Stuffed Pig's Feet

Golden Casserole

4 Pork in the Microwave Oven 124

The Humble Provider

The food of the common people rather than of kings, pork has for centuries been a dietary mainstay for millions worldwide. The reasons have much to do with economy: The pig is easy to raise, being omnivorous and requiring little land for grazing; and almost every part of its carcass can be eaten. However, two associated misconceptions—that the pig is by nature an unclean animal, and that its meat is only for those who cannot afford better fare—have tended in the past to obscure the virtues of pork: its distinctive flavor and its high level of nutritional benefits.

Our standard image of the pig—stocky, snub-nosed, its rounded bulk finished with the merest doodle of a tail—is itself somewhat out-of-date and misleading. This awkward, overloaded beast was first developed by progressive European stockbreeders of the 18th century, who aimed to produce an animal that would satisfy the high-energy dietary requirements of an active population. Since then, of course, our life-styles have in general become more sedentary and our eating habits have changed accordingly. Today's pig is bred more for its lean meat than for its fat. Rich in protein, minerals, and B vitamins—especially thiamine (vitamin B1), which is essential for the release of energy from carbohydrates—lean, fresh pork has much to contribute to a healthful diet.

Pork, fat, and cholesterol

A pig's carcass contains about 32 percent fat, and after all surface fat has been trimmed from fresh pork, the lean meat that remains contains an average of 7 percent fat (compared with 9 percent in lean lamb and 4.5 percent in lean beef). It is worth emphasizing that the strictures of modern nutritionists are directed not against fat itself but against the quantity of fat in our diet—and even if it were possible to eliminate fat altogether, this goal would not be desirable. Fat is an essential nutrient—especially for children—because it provides certain fat-soluble vitamins and helps the body to absorb these; it contains essentially fatty acids that the body cannot produce itself but that are converted by the body into the basic material of cell membranes; and it is the most concentrated source of energy available. In addition, fat contributes to flavor and palatability, and because it takes longer to digest than protein and carbohydrates, it is chiefly responsible for that comfortable feeling of satisfaction that comes after eating well.

Fat becomes culpable only when we eat too much of it—which most adults in the Western world tend to do. About 40 percent of our caloric intake is accounted for by fat, compared with about 10 percent in developing countries, and studies have shown that this high proportion is not only more than we need but is associated with the high incidence of obesity and coronary disease in the more affluent societies.

Closely linked with the issue of fat in the diet is that of the notorious compound cholesterol, which is present in pork in noticeable quantities. Excess cholesterol deposited within the walls of blood vessels can lead to circulatory problems and hence to arterial and heart disease, but the problem is not as simple as this connection implies. Present in all animal tissue, cholesterol is an organic fatty substance that is needed for the fluidity of our cell membranes and for the synthesis of certain hormones and vitamin D. The amount of cholesterol we take in with our food is normally far less than what is produced by the body itself and does not by itself raise the cholesterol in our blood to unacceptable levels. The villain is really saturated fat, which stimulates the body's own synthesis of cholesterol. (In contrast, polyunsaturated fats, present in certain plant and vegetable oils, can actually reduce cholesterol by aiding the body's mechanisms for getting rid of it.) For this reason, although it is sensible to be aware of the cholesterol levels in our diet and to eat cholesterol-rich foods such as liver and kidneys only occasionally, the main precaution we should take against raising the amount of cholesterol in our blood is to reduce our intake of fat, and especially of saturated fat.

What this means for the health-conscious cook is not that pork should be avoided, but rather that it should be cooked in new ways that capitalize on its benefits. The amounts of fat and cholesterol in each dish should be kept within reasonable limits, and the same principle applies to salt: Several studies have shown that for some people, excessive sodium intake may be linked with high blood pressure and strokes. It is the purpose of this book to show how these limits can be achieved without sacrifice to texture and taste.

Choosing the right ingredients

All the recipes in this book have been carefully developed to produce dishes that are both healthful in terms of their nutritional contents, and attractive, flavorful, and satisfying. To conform with these guidelines, the recipes concentrate on those cuts of pork that contain the least fat and sodium. The cuts most frequently called for are loin and tenderloin, both of which derive from the upper part of the carcass in which the proportion of fat to lean meat is relatively low. Belly and many of the other cuts *(page 10)* are generally too high in fat. Liver, brains, and kidneys are too high in cholesterol to be eaten more than occasionally, while cured meats—bacon and ham—are too high in sodium. The lean cuts are inevitably more expensive than the fatty cuts, but by restricting individual portions to no more than 3 ounces of cooked meat (based on 4 ounces of raw meat) and combining the meat with other appetizing ingredients that enhance its flavor, you can make each dish sufficiently economical to form part of an ordinary weekday meal.

Lovers of traditional pork recipes will be relieved to learn that not all of the cheaper cuts are outlawed, nor are patés and sausages and the special flavor of cured meat absolutely forbidden to the health-conscious eater. Meat from the shoulder, trimmed of all visible fat, is used in some of the stews, and in certain recipes you can substitute cheaper cuts of pork for the more expensive ones specified in the ingredients list—as long as you make allowance for the increased fat content when planning other dishes in the day's menu. This book includes recipes for a low-calorie terrine and for sausages made from lean ground pork with light, nutritious ingredients such as apples or potatoes in place of additional fat. Even ham, liver, and kidneys—used in moderate amounts and cooked with due care—are featured as primary ingredients.

The choice of ingredients that are cooked with the meat is in part determined by the need to cut down on fat and cholesterol. High-cholesterol dairy products such as cream and cheese should be used sparingly, or replaced with low-fat yogurt. There remains a vast range of healthful ingredients to choose from, many of them traditionally associated with pork in different national cuisines—for example, apples and cider in British dishes, fresh and dried fruit in French dishes, red and white cabbage in central European dishes, and chili peppers in Mexican dishes. Each in-gredient brings its own nutritional benefits to the assembled dish: Beans and dried fruit, for example, add fiber, while fresh fruit and vegetables are valuable sources of vitamins. A comparable range of herbs and spices, many of them also associated with particular cuisines, can be used to give piquancy to the meat in place of salt.

This list of ingredients at the head of each recipe in this book begins with the pork and continues with the remaining ingredients in order of use. For clarity, the ingredients for a self-sufficient part of the dish—such as a marinade, sauce, or pastry dough—may be listed separately. Many of the recipes conclude with a suggested accompaniment to the main dish.

Cooking pork the healthful way

The nutritional value of a dish is affected not only by the choice of raw ingredients but by the technique used to cook them. The recipes in this book are divided into four chapters according to the cooking methods employed: The first two chapters cover dry cooking (sautéing, broiling, roasting) and moist cooking (stewing, braising, and poaching and steaming). The third chapter contains a variety of less easily categorized methods, and the final chapter is devoted to cooking with a microwave oven. The introduction to each chapter includes hints and suggestions appropriate to the recipes that follow, but there a number of points about cooking pork in a healthful way that should be kept in mind whichever cooking method you employ.

To keep down calories and fat content, all surface fat should be trimmed from the meat with a sharp knife before it is cooked. For the same reason, the meat should be cooked in heavy-bottomed or nonstick pots or pans with the absolute minimum of cooking oil.

Fat that melts out of the meat during cooking should be discarded by a process known as skimming or degreasing. Use a soup ladle or a large, shallow spoon to skim off the fat that rises to the surface of the liquid in which the meat is being cooked; if necessary, tilt the pan or set it half off the heat so that the fat will collect on the still side of the pan. Small amounts of fat that remain can be removed with a paper towel: Lay a corner or strip of paper towel directly on the fat, then lift the towel away.

To prevent the meat from drying out during cooking—a role traditionally accomplished by the fat in the meat itself or by basting or larding with additional fat—a number of strategies are available. These include filling the meat with a moist stuffing that bastes the meat from within, and tenderizing the meat before it is cooked by pounding it flat or steeping it in a marinade. Typically, marinades contain an acid liquid—such as wine, lemon juice, or vinegar—which softens the meat fibers and allows the other ingredients to penetrate; because acids react with some metals to produce an unpleasant taste, the pork should always be marinated in a glass, enamel, or other nonreactive dish.

In dry cooking, the meat is first subjected to high heat to brown the surface, and then the heat is lowered to allow the center of the meat to cook through. The purpose of the initial searing is twofold: First, the outside of the meat undergoes complex chemical changes, known as browning reactions, that produce an intense, highly appetizing flavor; and second, an appealing crust is formed on the surface of the meat. To add color and flavor, meat that is to be braised or poached may also be browned over high heat or in the oven before the liquid is added.

One major health hazard associated with pork is trichinosis, caused by the ingestion of undercooked pork infected with tiny worms—*trichinae*—that burrow into the muscle of the pig and live in the human intestines. Invisible to the naked eye and capable of surviving both refrigeration and the heat of smoking, the worms can be destroyed only by thorough cooking. Although the number of pigs affected is extremely low, it is still worth taking elementary precautions: Do not taste uncooked pork— even to test a raw sausage mixture for flavor—and cook all pork until the juices are no longer pink. (This does not mean that pork should be overcooked.) Test small pieces of meat such as chops by pricking them with a skewer: If the juices that flow out are pink, the meat must be cooked longer. For larger pieces of pork, insert a meat thermometer into the thickest part of the meat, avoiding any bones, and cook until the internal temperature reaches 160° F.

Going back to nature

Most of the pork that is now sold in butchers' shops and supermarkets comes from animals that have been raised intensively on factory-like farms. In recent years, an increasing number of people—including both farmers and consumers—have become concerned about the possible side effects of this type of farming.

Whereas sheep are generally raised outdoors and cattle are kept outdoors for at least the summer months, most pigs are housed for all their lives in buildings where light and temperature are strictly controlled. They are routinely injected with antibiotics and have growth-promoting agents added to their feed, which itself derives from land treated with nitrates and pesticides. The humans who ultimately consume the meat of these animals ingest resistant strains of bacteria and chemical residues that can cause illnesses and allergic reactions.

In Europe and America, there are now associations of farmers dedicated to organic cultivation and the raising of animals by traditional methods. While exploiting the benefits of scientific progress where appropriate—for example, in the use of antibiotics to treat sick animals—these farmers do not use nitrates, pesticides, and other unnecessary chemicals, and they allow their animals to range freely in natural conditions. They take pains to spare the animals stress and injury during shipping and stress in the slaughterhouse.

Most of the farmers who adhere to the rules laid down by the various associations sell their produce by mail order or through specialty shops, and at present, their meat constitutes a very small proportion of the total market. However, it is worth seeking out for the sake of both health and flavor. Free-range pork costs more than meat from intensively reared pigs, but you are unlikely to regret the extra expense.

Buying and storing pork

Whether buying fresh pork from a specialty retailer such as those described above or from an ordinary butcher's shop or supermarket, look for firm, odorless, fine-textured meat. The flesh should be pale and pinkish, the fat white, and the bones tinged with red. Most pigs are slaughtered at the relatively young age of six to seven months; coarse-textured flesh and white, hard bones usually indicate an older animal.

Like other meats, pork should be stored in the refrigerator at a temperature of 40° F. or below. Ideally, the meat should be laid on a rack over a plate and covered with an upturned bowl so that moisture is retained but air can circulate around the meat. Ground pork will keep for one or two days under these conditions, whole pieces for three to four days. Cooked meat and leftovers should be wrapped tightly in plastic wrap or aluminum foil, and kept for no more than two days.

Freezing is not considered beneficial to pork: Its young, tender meat tends to harden, and freezer burn—surface discoloration and loss of nutritive value caused by drying out at low temperatures—can occur more quickly than with most other meats. If you do wish to store pork in the freezer, first trim off all visible fat, which can reduce storage life. Wrap the trimmed meat tightly in vapor-proof wrap or aluminum foil to prevent freezer burn and to keep out oxygen (which causes fat to become rancid). Keep the pork at a temperature of 0° F. or lower. Under these conditions, pork will keep from three to six months in the freezer. The meat can be transferred to the refrigerator one to two days before it is needed, to thaw gently; alternatively it can be thawed in a microwave oven. It should be kept covered during thawing and then cooked at once.

The Key to Better Eating

This book, like others in the Healthy Home Cooking series, presents an analysis of nutrients contained in a single serving of each dish, listed beside the recipe itself, as on the right. Approximate counts for calories, protein, cholesterol, total fat, saturated fat (the kind that increases the body's blood cholesterol), and sodium are given.

Healthy Home Cooking addresses the concerns of today's weight-conscious, health-minded cooks by providing recipes that take into account guidelines set by nutritionists. The secret of eating well, of course, has to do with maintaining a balance of foods in the diet; most of us consume too much sugar and salt, too much fat and too many calories, even too much protein.

Interpreting the chart

The chart at right shows the National Research Council's Recommended Dietary Allowances of calories and protein for healthy men, women, and children, along with the council's recommendations for the "safe and adequate" maximum intake of sodium. Although the council has not established recommendations for either cholesterol or fat, the chart does include what the National Institutes of Health and the American Heart Association consider the daily maximum amounts of these for healthy members of the general population. The Heart Association, among other concerned groups, has pointed out that Americans derive about 40 percent of their calories from fat; this, it believes, should be cut back to less than 30 percent.

The volumes in the Healthy Home Cooking series do not purport to be diet books, nor do they focus on health foods. Rather, they express a commonsense approach to cooking that uses salt, sugar, cream, butter, and oil in moderation while employing other ingredients that also provide flavor and satisfaction. Herbs, spices, aromatic vegetables, fruit, citrus zest, juices, wines, and vinegars are all used to achieve this end.

The recipes make few unusual demands.

Calories **250**
Protein **23g.**
Cholesterol **70mg.**
Total fat **11g.**
Saturated fat **3g.**
Sodium **185mg.**

Naturally, they call for fresh ingredients offering substitutes when these are unavailable. (The substitute is not calculated in the nutrient analysis, however.) Most of the ingredients can be found in any well-stocked supermarket; the occasional exception can be bought in specialty or ethnic shops. A glossary on pages 140 and 141 describes and defines ingredients that may be unfamiliar.

In Healthy Home Cooking's test kitchens, heavy-bottomed pots and pans are used to guard against burning the food whenever a small amount of oil is used, but nonstick pans could be utilized as well. Both safflower oil and virgin olive oil are favored for sautéing. Safflower was chosen because it is the most highly polyunsaturated vegetable fat available in supermarkets, and polyunsaturated fats reduce blood cholesterol; if unobtainable, use sunflower oil, also high in polyunsaturated fats. Virgin olive oil is used because it has a fine fruity flavor lacking in the lesser

grade known as "pure." In addition, it is—like all olive oil—high in monounsaturated fats, which are thought not to increase blood cholesterol. When virgin olive oil is unavailable, "pure" may be substituted.

About cooking times

To help the cook plan ahead effectively, Healthy Home Cooking takes time into account in all of its recipes. While recognizing that everyone cooks at a different speed and that stoves and ovens differ in temperatures, the series provides approximate "working" and "total" times for every dish. Working time denotes the actual minutes spent on preparation; total time includes unattended cooking time, as well as time devoted to marinating, steeping, or soaking. Since the recipes emphasize fresh foods, they may take a little longer to prepare than "quick and easy" dishes that call for canned or packaged products, but the payoff in flavor and often in nutrition should compensate for the extra time involved.

In order to simplify meal planning, most recipes list accompaniments. These are intended only as suggestions, however; cooks should let their imaginations be their guide and come up with their own ideas to achieve an appealing and sensible balance of foods.

Recommended Dietary Guidelines

		Average Daily Intake		Maximum Daily Intake			
		CALORIES	PROTEIN grams	CHOLESTEROL milligrams	TOTAL FAT grams	SATURATED FAT grams	SODIUM milligrams
Children	7-10	2400	22	240	80	27	1800
Females	11-14	2200	37	220	73	24	2700
	15-18	2100	44	210	70	23	2700
	19-22	2100	44	300	70	23	3300
	23-50	2000	44	300	67	22	3300
	51-75	1800	44	300	60	20	3300
Males	11-14	2700	36	270	90	30	2700
	15-18	2800	56	280	93	31	2700
	19-22	2900	56	300	97	32	3300
	23-50	2700	56	300	90	30	3300
	51-75	2400	56	300	80	27	3300

Techniques for Quality Cuts

For many of the dishes in this book, the cook's first task is preparing the meat—boning, trimming, slicing, chopping, or flattening according to the requirements of the specific recipe. No professional expertise is necessary, but each job can be carried out most efficiently by following a logical sequence of steps. The techniques shown on the opposite page and overleaf will help you prepare successful dishes with a minimum of waste.

Lean ground pork can be ordered specially from your butcher, of course. The only way to ensure a truly lean product with precisely the consistency you require, however, is to prepare the meat yourself. This can be done with a meat grinder or a food processor, or by finely chopping by hand (opposite, top); the latter technique will retain more of the meat's juices. The meat shown in the demonstration is pork tenderloin, which is specified in a number of recipes that call for lean ground pork, but other lean cuts can be ground in the same way after they have been trimmed of fat.

The tender meat of the tenderloin makes it an appropriate cut for all of the dry cooking methods that are employed in Chapter 1. Sliced lengthwise and flattened out with a wooden mallet (opposite, bottom), the tenderloin can be rolled around a prepared filling and roasted. And, cut into regular slices that are then tenderized by pounding (technique, page 12), the tenderloin yields cutlets of pork for frying or broiling.

Chops and loin steaks are usually fried or broiled, and they provide a quick, easy meal for a family lunch or supper. Several of the recipes in this book, however, show you how to transform these simple cuts into more special dishes by stuffing them with apple slices (page 19), fennel leaves (page 95), pine nuts and rice (page 126), and a number of other fillings. Making the pocket that holds the stuffing requires only a few deft turns with a sharp knife (technique, page 12).

Boning a whole loin of pork may appear to be a more ambitious procedure, but this too requires only a quickly learned dexterity with a sharp knife. The middle loin cut shown in the demonstration on page 13 contains the tenderloin. The rib bones—which must be cut free from the meat and snapped off—and the vertebrae, which make up the spinal column, can be used to make stock. The boned loin may be rolled around a stuffing—such as the pureed fava beans and yogurt on page 50—and roasted. It can also be braised in the oven—as in pork cooked like game (page 73), where the meat is first marinated in a mixture of wine, herbs, and juniper berries.

In all the techniques shown, good-quality kitchen knives with sharpened blades are essential. Hone the blades on a sharpening steel before using them, and wipe them clean after every use. Always place the meat that is to be cut or chopped on a scrupulously clean cutting board.

A Guide to Pork Cuts

This diagram identifies the primal cuts into which the pig's carcass is divided and lists the main retail cuts derived from them. The proportion of lean meat to fat is highest in the loin (colored area), the source of the pork used in most of the recipes in this book.

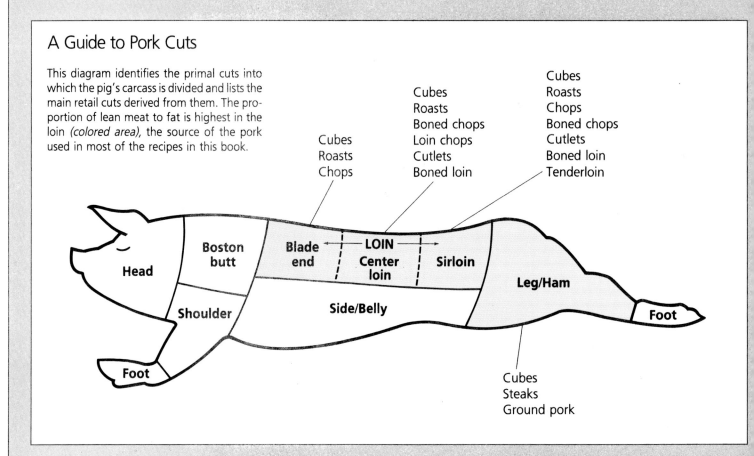

Trimming and Chopping a Tenderloin

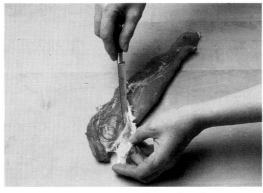

1 *PEELING THE MEMBRANE. Lift an edge of membrane with your fingers and start to peel it away from the meat, lightly pressing the knife blade down the underside of the membrane and against the meat. Discard each strip as it comes free.*

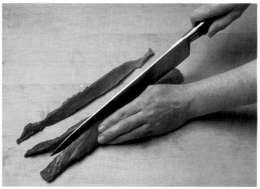

2 *CUTTING INTO STRIPS. Lay the tenderloin on a cutting surface, one short end toward you, and using a sharp knife, cut it lengthwise into strips about ⅓ inch wide. Then cut across the strips to make cubes.*

3 *CHOPPING. Spread the cubes out evenly on the cutting surface. Use a matched pair of sharp, heavy knives to chop the meat; let the blades fall alternately onto the meat, using your wrists to control the knives, as if beating a drum (above, left). From time to time, slide the blade of one knife under the meat and fold the meat back on itself (above, right). Continue chopping and folding until the meat is consistently and finely chopped.*

Flattening a Tenderloin

1 *SLICING OPEN THE TENDERLOIN. Trim all visible fat and membrane. Steady the tenderloin with your free hand, and use a long, sharp knife to cut it lengthwise to a depth of about 1½ inches. Lift the upper section of the tenderloin with your free hand and deepen the cut to within ⅓ inch of the opposite side.*

2 *FLATTENING THE TENDERLOIN. Open out the tenderloin into a rectangular shape and lay it on a sheet of plastic wrap. Cover the tenderloin with a second sheet of plastic wrap. Using the flat, wide side of a wooden mallet, pound the tenderloin to the thickness required for the recipe.*

Making Cutlets from Pork Tenderloin

1 *CUTTING ON THE DIAGONAL. Trim all visible fat and membrane from the tenderloin with a sharp knife (technique, page 11). Working from the thick end and holding the knife at an angle of 45 degrees to the tenderloin, cut off the number of slices required.*

2 *POUNDING CUTLETS. Place the slices on a sheet of plastic wrap, then lay another sheet of plastic wrap on top. Using the flat, wide side of a wooden mallet, pound the slices firmly until they are the size and thickness required.*

Preparing and Stuffing a Chop

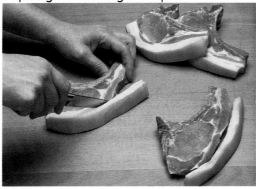

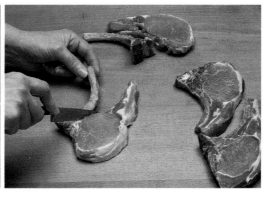

1 *TRIMMING OFF THE FAT. Working from the narrow end of the chop, use a sharp knife to trim off the band of fat. Take care not to cut into the flesh with the blade of the knife.*

2 *BONING THE CHOP. Again working from the narrow end of the chop, use the knife to separate the rib bone from the flesh, pulling away the bone with your free hand as you cut. At the thick end, use the point of the blade to cut and twist away the bone.*

3 *MAKING THE POCKET. Cut a shallow slit about 1½ inches long in the rounded side of the chop. Press the knife blade deeper into the chop and work it backward and forward to hollow out a deep, wide pocket that extends almost to the edges of the meat.*

4 *STUFFING THE CHOP. Open up the slit in the rounded side of the chop with the fingers and thumb of your free hand, and fill the pocket with the prepared stuffing. Press the stuffing firmly into the chop to distribute it evenly.*

Boning a Loin

1 LOOSENING THE RIBS. To loosen each rib, first cut along both sides of the rib, being careful not to cut into the flesh any deeper than necessary. Then press the rib upward and cut underneath it toward the spine.

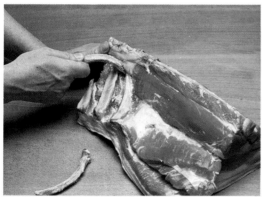

2 DETACHING THE RIBS. Holding the loin steady with your free hand, grip the end of a rib with your thumb and forefinger, and twist it to sever it from the spine. If the bone is slippery, grip it with wax paper. Remove the other ribs in the same way.

3 RELEASING THE TENDERLOIN. Keeping the knife blade close to the bone, cut along the spine to release the tenderloin. As the connective tissue is severed, the tenderloin will fall away from the spine.

4 LOOSENING THE SPINE. Feel with your fingers where the extensions of the vertebrae protrude into the flesh. Cut around and under the extensions to free them from the flesh.

5 CUTTING AWAY THE SPINE. Work the blade of the knife underneath the spine along its entire length, using your free hand to pull the spine away from the flesh as you proceed.

1 *Lean pork chops are marinated in a paste of yogurt, turmeric, and Indian spices before being cooked under a broiler (recipe, page 37).*

Simple Succulence

Cooking by direct heat—or, in the case of frying, by the transfer of heat from the pan—is the simplest and oldest method of preparing fresh pork for the table. For frying and grilling or broiling, the meat must be thin enough to cook through before the surface burns—chops, cutlets, and steaks are suitable candidates for these methods. For roasting, which cooks the meat more slowly, larger cuts such as whole loin or tenderloin are more appropriate, but for all dry cooking methods you should select tender meat containing little connective tissue.

In traditional pork recipes, fat plays an important role in keeping the meat moist during cooking—a roast, for example, might be basted with its own juices and liquid fat, a lean joint might be barded with fat or threaded with lardoons, and cubes of meat might be alternated on skewers for grilling with pieces of fatty bacon. Because very little cooking oil is used in the recipes in this chapter, and because the pork itself is trimmed of fat before cooking, a certain amount of ingenuity is required to keep the meat from drying out.

To reduce the cooking time required, pork that is to be fried, broiled, or grilled can first be tenderized by pounding with a mallet, or by steeping in a marinade. For Oriental stir-fried dishes, the meat is cut into thin strips that can be cooked through in as little as 15 seconds. In the recipe for crepinettes on page 56, the oval patties are wrapped in caul, a thin membrane of fat from the pig's stomach that melts and moistens the meat. For roasts, the meat may be stuffed with moist ingredients that release flavorful juices during cooking. Or the meat may be roasted with a little liquid poured around it—such as the wine, lemon juice, and chopped tomatoes in the Cretan roast on page 58.

In many of the recipes, the browned bits that remain on the bottom of the pan after the meat has been sautéed are incorporated into a sauce by deglazing the pan with a liquid such as wine, stock, or fruit juice, and then simmering this liquid with additional ingredients. If the meat has first been marinated, the reserved marinade is often added to the pan at this stage. Reduced by rapid boiling or thickened with a little arrowroot, the sauce is poured around or over the meat on the serving dish. While this sauce is being prepared, the simplest way to keep the meat warm is to place it in a low oven in a dish loosely covered with aluminum foil.

After roasting, larger pieces of meat should be left to rest for about 10 minutes before serving. During dry cooking, the blood and juices in the meat tend to concentrate in the center, and they will run out if the meat is carved immediately; the resting time allows the juices to circulate evenly and the meat to become firm.

Tea Chops with Two Purees

Serves 4
Working time: about 40 minutes
Total time: about 3 hours (includes marinating)

Calories **340**
Protein **36g.**
Cholesterol **70mg.**
Total fat **11g.**
Saturated fat **5g.**
Sodium **310mg.**

8 boned pork chops (about 4 oz. each), trimmed of fat
8 shallots, finely chopped
½ cup red wine
2 cups unsalted chicken or veal stock (recipes, page 139)
½ lb. sweet potatoes
¾ lb. broccoli florets
½ cup plain low-fat yogurt
½ tsp. salt
freshly ground black pepper
Cardamom marinade
5 tbsp. unsalted chicken or veal stock (recipes, page 139), or water
2½ tsp. strong Indian tea leaves, or a tea bag
32 cardamom pods
½ lemon, grated zest only
½ tsp. salt
freshly ground black pepper

To make the marinade, bring the stock or water to a boil. Remove it from the heat, add the tea leaves or tea bag, and cover for three minutes. Strain the liquid into a bowl, add the cardamom pods, lemon zest, salt, and some pepper, and cover for 20 to 30 minutes.

Remove the cardamom pods from the tea mixture and press them with the back of a spoon until they open; scrape out the seeds and crush them lightly with the spoon, then return both pods and seeds to the liquid. Place the pork in a large, shallow dish, pour the marinade over it, cover the dish with plastic wrap, and set it aside to marinate in a cool place for two hours, turning the meat once.

When the meat has marinated for an hour and a half, cook the shallots in a nonstick saucepan until they are translucent, then add the wine and simmer until almost all of the wine has evaporated. Pour in the stock, bring the liquid to a boil, lower the heat, and simmer to reduce it by half—15 to 20 minutes.

Remove the chops from the marinade and pat them dry with paper towels. Strain the marinade; reserve some of the cardamom pods for a garnish.

Add half of the strained marinade to the reduced sauce base, bring it to a boil, then simmer to reduce it until it has a light syrupy consistency. Add more of the marinade to achieve the desired consistency. Strain the sauce through a fine-mesh sieve and keep it warm.

In a dry, heavy-bottomed nonstick frying pan, sear the meat over high heat for two minutes on each side. Lower the heat and continue to cook for 10 minutes more, turning once. Remove the meat from the pan and put it in a warm oven to rest for a few minutes.

Meanwhile, steam or boil the sweet potatoes and broccoli in separate saucepans until they are tender. Puree the vegetables separately in a food processor or a food mill. Blend half of the yogurt and salt into each

puree, and add some pepper; sieve the mixtures if a smoother texture is preferred. If either puree appears too runny, cook it in a saucepan over low heat to evaporate some of the liquid.

Transfer the purees to serving bowls. Place two chops on each diner's plate, pour a little sauce over them, and garnish with the reserved cardamom pods.

EDITOR'S NOTE: *Other vegetables of contrasting taste and color may be used instead of the sweet potatoes and broccoli—for example, Brussels sprouts and rutabagas, or spinach and carrots.*

Chops with Cranberry Sauce

Serves 4
Working (and total) time: about 20 minutes

Calories **245**	
Protein **29g.**	4 pork chops (4½ to 5 oz. each), trimmed of fat
Cholesterol **60mg.**	1 cup cranberries
Total fat **9g.**	¾ cup unsalted chicken stock (recipe, page 139) or water
Saturated fat **4g.**	freshly ground black pepper
Sodium **270mg.**	½ tbsp. safflower oil
	½ tsp. salt
	2 tbsp. red-currant jelly

To make the sauce, put the cranberries into a small saucepan with the stock or water, and cook over medium-low heat until the skins begin to split—about

three minutes. Reserve a few whole cranberries for a garnish and rub the rest through a sieve. Discard the skins left in the sieve and reserve the sieved liquid.

Rub both sides of each chop with some pepper. Heat the oil in a heavy-bottomed frying pan over high heat, and when it is hot, add the chops. Sear them on both sides and immediately lower the heat. Cook over medium heat, turning occasionally, until the meat is firm but still springy to the touch—about seven minutes. Remove the chops from the pan, season them with half of the salt, and keep them warm.

Add the cranberry puree and the jelly to the pan, and reduce until the sauce is slightly syrupy—about one minute; add the remaining salt. Serve the chops with the sauce and the reserved whole cranberries spooned around them.

Stuffed Pork Chops with Calvados

Serves 4
Working time: about 30 minutes
Total time: about 45 minutes

Calories **375**
Protein **29g.**
Cholesterol **70mg.**
Total fat **14g.**
Saturated fat **4g.**
Sodium **270mg.**

4 boned pork chops (4½ to 5 oz. each), trimmed of fat
3 apples
1 tbsp. finely chopped fresh thyme, or 1 tsp. dried thyme leaves
freshly ground black pepper
3 tbsp. fresh lemon juice
1½ tbsp. safflower oil
½ cup Calvados
1½ tbsp. light cream
½ tsp. salt

Make a small incision in the side of each chop and carefully cut a pocket *(technique, page 12)*. Peel, core, and thinly slice one apple, sprinkle half of the thyme over the slices, and press them into the pockets in the chops. Season the chops with some pepper, rubbing it in with your fingers. Peel and core the remaining apples, then cut them into rings, and sprinkle the rings with the lemon juice to prevent them from discoloring.

Heat half of the oil in a heavy-bottomed skillet over high heat. When it is hot but not smoking, add the chops and brown them for one minute on each side. Remove the pan from the heat and allow the chops to sizzle for three minutes more, turning them once. Remove the chops from the pan and keep them warm.

Heat the remaining oil in the skillet over medium heat, and add the apples and the remaining thyme. Cook over low heat until the apples are almost soft—three to five minutes. Remove the pan from the heat. Add the Calvados, and when the sizzling has stopped, return the pan to the heat and cook for another minute. Add the cream and allow the mixture to bubble up once. Replace the chops in the pan, pouring in any juices that have collected; stir in the salt, warm through, and serve.

SUGGESTED ACCOMPANIMENT: *parslied carrots.*

Stir-Fried Pork and Squid

Serves 4
Working time: about 15 minutes
Total time: about 1 hour (includes marinating)

Calories **200**
Protein **23g.**
Cholesterol **205mg.**
Total fat **10g.**
Saturated fat **2g.**
Sodium **320mg.**

½ lb. pork tenderloin, trimmed of fat and cut into thin strips
½ lb. squid, cleaned and cut into thin strips
1 tbsp. low-sodium soy sauce
1 tbsp. dry sherry
16 scallions
1 tsp. cornstarch
4 tbsp. unsalted vegetable or chicken stock (recipes, page 139), or water
1 tbsp. safflower oil
1 tsp. sesame oil
2 tsp. finely chopped fresh ginger

Place the pork and squid in a nonreactive dish with the soy sauce and sherry to marinate for 45 minutes.

Cut the scallions into 2-inch pieces; reserve some of the green tops and slice them into julienne for garnish.

Remove the pork and squid from the marinade, and set them aside. Mix the cornstarch and the stock or water into the marinade.

Heat a wok or a heavy-bottomed skillet over high heat, and add the safflower and the sesame oil. Add the ginger and stir-fry for one minute. Add the pork and squid, and stir-fry for four minutes; then add the scallion pieces and cook for two minutes. Pour in the marinade mixture, cook for one minute more, and serve at once, garnished with the scallion julienne.

Stir-Fried Pork with Snow Peas

Serves 2
Working time: about 30 minutes
Total time: about 50 minutes (includes marinating)

Calories **135**
Protein **14g.**
Cholesterol **175mg.**
Total fat **4g.**
Saturated fat **2g.**
Sodium **220mg.**

½ lb. pork tenderloin, trimmed of fat and cut into ¼-inch-thick strips
5 dried shiitake mushrooms, soaked in hot water for 20 to 30 minutes
12 frozen baby corn
3 scallions
2 tsp. safflower oil
1 garlic clove, crushed
½-inch piece fresh ginger, cut into fine julienne
½ cup bamboo shoots, thinly sliced lengthwise
½ lb. snow peas, strings removed
1 tsp. low-sodium soy sauce
1 tsp. dry or medium-dry sherry
2 tbsp. unsalted chicken or veal stock (recipes, page 139), or 2 tbsp. water
1 tsp. cornstarch, mixed with 4 tsp. cold water
1 small carrot, cut into fine julienne

Sherry marinade
1 tsp. low-sodium soy sauce
1 tsp. dry or medium-dry sherry
1 tsp. cornstarch
ground white pepper

To prepare the marinade, mix together the soy sauce, sherry, cornstarch, and some white pepper in a non-reactive dish. Add the pork strips and toss them well to coat them evenly, then allow them to marinate for 15 to 20 minutes.

Meanwhile, strain the mushroom-soaking liquid through cheesecloth and reserve it; squeeze the mushrooms dry and slice them thinly. Blanch the corn for five minutes in a pan of lightly salted boiling water with a squeeze of lemon juice added, then refresh it in cold water and drain. Shred the scallions finely along the grain and put the strips into a bowl of ice water; when the strips have curled, drain them.

Heat 1 teaspoon of the oil in a wok or a large, deep frying pan over medium high until it is hot but not smoking, then stir-fry the pork strips until they are light brown—about two minutes. Remove the pork strips from the wok and drain them in a sieve set over a bowl.

Wipe the wok clean with paper towels, then heat

the remaining oil and add the garlic. Discard the garlic when it is brown, and add the ginger, bamboo shoots, and mushrooms. Stir-fry for three minutes, then add the snow peas and stir-fry for another three minutes.

Lower the heat, and add the soy sauce, sherry, stock or water, reserved mushroom-soaking liquid, and any meat juices from the pork strips. Increase the heat and cook for another two to three minutes; then add the cornstarch mixture, and stir until the sauce thickens and turns translucent. Add the pork strips and the corn to the wok, and heat them for one minute; remove the wok from the heat and stir in the carrot julienne.

Serve the finished dish from the wok with the scallion curls sprinkled over it.

SUGGESTED ACCOMPANIMENT: *plain boiled rice.*

Pork and Ginger Stir-Fry Salad

Serves 4
Working time: about 35 minutes
Total time: about 50 minutes

Calories **235**
Protein **23g.**
Cholesterol **70mg.**
Total fat **14g.**
Saturated fat **4g.**
Sodium **205mg.**

1 lb. pork tenderloin, trimmed of fat and cut into thin strips
1 tbsp. sesame oil
1 garlic clove, crushed
1-inch piece fresh ginger, finely chopped
1 tsp. chili sauce
2 tbsp. low-sodium soy sauce
3 shallots, thinly sliced
1/8 tsp. Chinese five-spice powder
1 tbsp. safflower oil
1 sweet red pepper, seeded, deribbed, and cut into thin strips
Lettuce and bean-sprout salad
1/2 small head red oakleaf lettuce, washed and dried
6 curly endive leaves, washed and dried
1 bunch watercress, washed and stalks trimmed
4 Nappa cabbage leaves, washed, dried, and shredded
4 scallions, sliced diagonally
1 cup bean sprouts

To make the marinade, mix the sesame oil with the garlic, ginger, chili sauce, soy sauce, shallots, and five-spice powder in a large, nonreactive bowl. Add the pork strips and mix well. Cover and marinate for at least 15 minutes.

Meanwhile, prepare the salad. Arrange the oakleaf lettuce, curly endive leaves, and watercress sprigs in a border around a serving dish. Mix the shredded Nappa cabbage with the scallions and bean sprouts, and place the mixture in the center of the dish.

Heat the oil in a wok or a large, heavy-bottomed skillet. Add the pork and its marinade, and cook for four minutes, stirring all the time. Add the pepper strips and cook for one to two minutes more, stirring constantly; then pile the hot pork mixture over the salad and serve at once.

Stir-Fried Liver in Orange and Brandy Sauce

Serves 4
Working (and total) time: about 15 minutes

Calories **340**	¾ lb. pork liver, thinly sliced
Protein **29g.**	2 tbsp. safflower oil
Cholesterol **235mg.**	2 onions, sliced
Total fat **18g.**	1 green pepper, seeded, deribbed, and sliced
Saturated fat **5g.**	1 garlic clove, chopped
Sodium **290mg.**	1 tbsp. all-purpose flour
	2 tbsp. tomato paste
	3 oranges, two peeled, halved lengthwise, and sliced crosswise, juice only of the third
	½ cup unsalted vegetable stock (recipe, page 139)
	½ tsp. salt
	freshly ground black pepper
	2 tbsp. brandy
	3 tbsp. light cream (optional)

Heat the oil in a wok or a large, heavy-bottomed skillet and cook the liver over medium-high heat until it has colored—three to four minutes. Remove the liver from the pan and set it aside.

Put the onions, green pepper, and garlic into the pan, and cook over low heat until soft—five to 10 minutes. Stir in the flour and tomato paste, gradually add the orange juice and stock, and add the salt and some pepper. Bring to a boil, stirring constantly.

Reserve a few orange slices for a garnish; add the remaining slices to the pan along with the cooked liver and the brandy, and cook for one minute to heat through. Remove the pan from the heat and stir in the cream, if you are using it. Serve garnished with the reserved orange slices.

SUGGESTED ACCOMPANIMENT: *plain boiled rice.*

Loire Cutlets

Serves 4
Working time: about 20 minutes
Total time: about 40 minutes

Calories **310**
Protein **19g.**
Cholesterol **75mg.**
Total fat **9g.**
Saturated fat **4g.**
Sodium **290mg.**

4 pork cutlets (about 4 oz. each), trimmed of fat
½ tsp. salt
freshly ground black pepper
8 peeled shallots
1 cup Sancerre, Sauvignon, or other Loire wine
4 black peppercorns
1 sprig tarragon
½ tsp. unsalted butter
1 tsp. sugar
1 tsp. virgin olive oil
½ cup black seedless grapes, or other black grapes, halved and seeded
½ cup green seedless grapes, or other green grapes, halved and seeded
½ tsp. arrowroot
⅓ cup unsweetened grape juice or unsalted veal stock (recipe, page 139)
1 tbsp. finely chopped fresh tarragon
1 tbsp. finely chopped fresh chervil or parsley

Pound the cutlets to tenderize them *(page 12, Step 2)*, rub them with the salt and some pepper, and set aside.

In a heavy, nonreactive saucepan, simmer the shallots in half the wine, with the peppercorns and the sprig of tarragon, until they are soft—about 20 minutes—then add the butter and sugar, and toss over medium-high heat until all the liquid has evaporated and the shallots are lightly caramelized. Remove the shallots from the pan and reserve them. Discard the tarragon and peppercorns; deglaze the saucepan with a few tablespoons of the wine, and set it aside.

Heat the oil in a heavy, nonstick frying pan over medium-high heat. Cook the cutlets until they are brown—about two minutes on each side; ensure that the meat is cooked through, but do not overcook. Remove the meat from the pan and keep it warm.

Deglaze the pan with a few spoonfuls of the remaining wine; add the wine mixture from the shallot saucepan, and allow the sauce to reduce for a moment; finally, add the rest of the wine, with the grapes and shallots, and warm through. Dissolve the arrowroot in 1 tablespoon of the grape juice or stock, stir this into the rest of the grape juice or stock, and add it to the wine and grapes. Bring to a boil, stirring constantly, and simmer until the sauce is slightly thickened and translucent—about one minute.

Return the cutlets to the pan to warm through, then stir in the chopped tarragon and chervil or parsley, and serve immediately.

Caper Cutlets

Serves 4
Working (and total) time: about 20 minutes

Calories **190**
Protein **20g.**
Cholesterol **60mg.**
Total fat **10g.**
Saturated fat **4g.**
Sodium **260mg.**

4 pork cutlets (about 3½ oz. each), trimmed of fat
½ tsp. salt
freshly ground black pepper
cayenne pepper (optional)
2 tsp. dry mustard
1 tsp. safflower oil
2 tbsp. Marsala
1 orange, grated zest of half, juice of whole
1 tbsp. capers, rinsed, drained, and chopped
1 tsp. green peppercorns in brine, rinsed and drained
1 tsp. ground cinnamon
2 tbsp. sour cream
½ cup plain low-fat yogurt

Pound the cutlets to tenderize them *(page 12, Step 2)*, season with the salt and some black pepper, and some cayenne, if you wish; dust them with the mustard.

Brush a heavy-bottomed, nonstick skillet with the oil and heat the pan over medium-high heat. Brown the cutlets briefly and cook them for two minutes on each side; ensure that the meat is cooked through, but do not overcook. Remove the cutlets from the pan and keep them warm.

Deglaze the pan with the Marsala and cook until the wine is almost evaporated. Add the orange juice and zest to the pan, and reduce until it is syrupy. Stir in the capers, peppercorns, cinnamon, and sour cream, bring to a simmer, and cook for one minute. Remove the pan from the heat and stir in the yogurt. Return the pan to the heat to warm the yogurt, but do not allow the sauce to boil. Serve the cutlets with the sauce at once.

SUGGESTED ACCOMPANIMENT: *herbed potatoes.*

Tenderloin with Mushrooms and Water Chestnuts

Serves 4
Working time: about 30 minutes
Total time: about 1 hour and 30 minutes (includes chilling)

Calories **275**
Protein **24g.**
Cholesterol **70mg.**
Total fat **10g.**
Saturated fat **4g.**
Sodium **290mg.**

1 lb. pork tenderloin, trimmed of fat
3½ oz. water chestnuts, fresh or canned
1 cup unsalted vegetable stock (recipe, page 139), reduced to ⅔ cup
½ lb. button mushrooms, finely sliced

4 tbsp. dry white wine
1 tsp. fresh lemon juice
2-inch piece fresh ginger
1 tbsp. safflower oil
2 garlic cloves, crushed
½ tsp. salt
freshly ground black pepper
3 tbsp. sour cream
½ cup plain low-fat yogurt
finely chopped fresh chives or scallions for garnish (optional)

Chill the tenderloin in the freezer for one hour to make

it easier to cut, then slice it into very thin rounds.

If you are using fresh water chestnuts, scrub and peel them; canned chestnuts will already be peeled. Slice the chestnuts into thin rounds.

In a pan, simmer the water-chestnut slices in the reduced stock for 10 minutes, to allow them to absorb its flavor. In another pan, cook the mushrooms in the wine and lemon juice over medium heat for two minutes. Drain the chestnuts and mushrooms, reserving their cooking liquids separately, and set them aside.

Cut the ginger into four or five pieces, and use a garlic press to extract the juice, or grate the ginger and press it through a fine sieve; discard the ginger solids. In a frying pan, heat half of the oil with one of the garlic cloves and about one-third of the ginger juice over low heat for a minute or two, then discard the garlic and increase the heat to medium high.

Season the meat with the salt and some pepper, and quickly arrange about half of the slices in the hot frying pan. When the upper surface of each slice is nearly translucent—30 to 45 seconds—turn and brown the other side. Lift the slices out of the pan and keep them warm. Heat the rest of the oil with the remaining garlic

clove and one-third of the ginger juice as before, and brown the remaining slices of pork.

Once all the meat is cooked, gently wipe excess fat from the frying pan with a paper towel, but retain any browned bits and deglaze the pan over medium-high heat with the wine used to cook the mushrooms. When the wine has all but boiled away, add the stock used to cook the water chestnuts and reduce this mixture until it is slightly syrupy in appearance. Add the sour cream to the pan and cook the sauce for a few seconds more.

Strain the sauce through a fine-mesh sieve and wipe out the pan. Return the sauce to the pan, along with the meat, water chestnuts, and mushrooms. Heat the pan over low heat to warm all the ingredients, then stir in the yogurt, and continue to heat for another 30 seconds—do not allow the mixture to boil, as this will cause the sauce to separate.

Stir in the remaining ginger juice and serve the dish immediately, lightly sprinkled with the chives or scallions, if you are using them.

SUGGESTED ACCOMPANIMENTS: *plain brown rice; snow peas.*

Pork Saltimbocca

ALTHOUGH TRADITIONALLY MADE WITH THIN SLICES
OF VEAL, THIS ITALIAN DISH TASTES EQUALLY GOOD WHEN
MADE WITH LEAN PORK.

Serves 4
Working (and total) time: about 20 minutes

Calories **200**
Protein **22g.**
Cholesterol **70mg.**
Total fat **10g.**
Saturated fat **4g.**
Sodium **210mg.**

4 pork cutlets (about 4 oz. each), trimmed of fat
1 tbsp. grainy mustard
2 slices prosciutto (about ¾ oz. each)
12 small fresh sage leaves
1 tsp. unsalted butter
4 tbsp. Marsala
balsamic vinegar (optional)
freshly ground black pepper

Pound the cutlets firmly with a mallet until they have doubled in size *(page 12, Step 2)*. Spread the mustard over one surface of each cutlet. Place one slice of prosciutto over the mustard on each of two cutlets; divide the sage leaves between the other cutlets and press them firmly into the mustard.

Press each prosciutto-covered cutlet onto an herb-covered cutlet to make two sandwiches with a pro-sciutto and herb filling. Using a very sharp knife, cut each sandwich into six pieces.

If you have a large enough frying pan, cook in a single batch; otherwise, cook in two batches, dividing the butter accordingly. Melt the butter over medium-high heat until it is sizzling. Quickly, but carefully, place the cutlet sandwiches in the pan and cook until the centers are no longer pink—about one minute. Turn with a spatula and cook the second side for another 30 to 45 seconds. Pour the Marsala into the pan and allow it to reduce by half—about 30 seconds. Stir in some balsamic vinegar, if you wish, and add some black pepper. Serve the saltimbocca immediately.

SUGGESTED ACCOMPANIMENT: *crisp, colorful salad with balsamic vinaigrette.*

EDITOR'S NOTE: *Watercress leaves, in more generous quantity, may be substituted for the sage leaves. Smaller saltimbocca can be made using 1 pound of trimmed pork tenderloin, cut into 16 slices and pounded.*

Medallions of Pork with Two Green Purees

Serves 4
Working time: about 1 hour
Total time: about 7 hours (includes marinating)

Calories **290**
Protein **25g.**
Cholesterol **70mg.**
Total fat **18g.**
Saturated fat **4g.**
Sodium **185mg.**

1 lb. pork tenderloin, trimmed of fat
1 large green pepper, seeded, deribbed, and sliced
2 tsp. green peppercorns packed in brine, rinsed and drained
1½-inch piece fresh ginger, grated
2 tbsp. virgin olive oil
1 tbsp. wine vinegar
¼ tsp. salt
1 lb. fresh gooseberries
2 sprigs fresh mint
1 tbsp. sugar
2 cups fresh spinach
⅔ cup plain low-fat yogurt

Using a sharp knife, slice the tenderloin into ¼-inch-thick rounds, then pound them out until they are about half again as large *(technique, page 12)*.

Combine the green pepper, peppercorns, two-thirds of the ginger, 1 tablespoon of the oil, and the vinegar and salt in a food processor. (Or chop the green pepper and ginger, and then pound them and the peppercorns, oil, vinegar, and salt in a mortar.) Coat the pieces of meat with this marinade and let them marinate in a nonreactive dish for about six hours in a cool place (or 12 hours in the refrigerator).

To prepare the two purees, first wash and cook the gooseberries in a little water with the mint and sugar until they are soft. Drain the cooked gooseberries and pass them through a sieve, or puree them in a food processor or a blender; there is no need to stem the berries prior to sieving. If using a processor or a blender—which gives a creamy texture to the puree—sieve the puree after processing.

Wash the spinach and strip the leaves from the stalks. Cook the leaves with a little additional water until they are broken down and almost pureed. Beat the spinach into the yogurt, and using a garlic press, squeeze the juice from the remaining fresh ginger into the mixture. Keep the two purees warm in bowls set in pans of simmering water.

Wipe the marinade ingredients off the meat, which should be pale and tender. It does not matter if a little of the pepper mixture adheres to the meat—the brief cooking time will not allow this to burn. Heat half of the remaining oil in a large, heavy-bottomed skillet and cook half of the meat over low heat for up to one minute on each side; browning is not essential. Remove the cooked meat from the pan and keep it warm while the second batch cooks in the remaining oil.

Serve the medallions immediately, accompanied by the two purees.

SUGGESTED ACCOMPANIMENT: *snow peas or a green salad.*

EDITOR'S NOTE: *If you need to reheat the purees when the meat is ready to serve, the addition of a little arrowroot will prevent the spinach-yogurt mixture from separating.*

Homemade Pork Sausages

COMMERCIALLY MADE SAUSAGES CONTAIN A HIGH PROPORTION OF FAT. IN THESE TWO VERSIONS OF ONE RECIPE, THE FAT CONTENT IS LESS THAN 17 PERCENT.

Serves 10 (makes about 20 sausages)
Working time: about 1 hour
Total time: about 2 hours

Calories **300**
Protein **14g.**
Cholesterol **60mg.**
Total fat **24g.**
Saturated fat **9g.**
Sodium **280mg.**

2 lb. pork shoulder, trimmed of excess fat
3 to 3½ yards natural lamb sausage casings, soaked in acidulated water for about 1 hour
Seasonings for "Irish" sausages
2 cups mashed or diced cooked potato
2 tbsp. whiskey
1 tsp. ground white pepper
2 tsp. salt
1 tsp. yellow mustard seeds
1 tsp. ground caraway seeds
2 tsp. finely chopped fresh thyme
1 tsp. finely chopped fresh sage
Seasonings for "French" sausages
2 tart cooking apples, peeled, cored, chopped, and steamed until soft
1 tbsp. Calvados or cognac
1 tsp. ground allspice
4 tsp. finely chopped fresh basil
2 tsp. finely chopped fresh marjoram
1 tsp. finely chopped fresh mint
2 tsp. salt

Dice the meat and pass it through the medium blade of a meat grinder, or chop it finely in a food processor. Mix the meat with all the Irish or French seasoning ingredients, according to the type of sausage you have chosen to make, and pass it through the grinder or process it again. Cook 1 or 2 teaspoons of the mixture in a dry, nonstick pan for two to three minutes, then adjust the herb and spice seasonings of the rest of the sausage mixture as required.

Prepare the sausage casings according to the technique demonstrated at top right *(Step 1)*, and then fill the casings using the method described in Step 2. (If you are using a food processor or if your sausage-making equipment differs from the one illustrated here, be sure to follow the manufacturer's instructions.) Next, form the sausage links *(Step 3)*.

Before cooking, separate the sausage links and moisten the casings, but do not pierce them. Place the sausages in a nonstick frying pan and add cold water to cover the bottom of the pan. Bring the water to a boil and allow it to evaporate, then reduce the heat and cook the sausages over low heat, turning them by shaking the pan or by using a spatula, until they are brown all over—about 15 minutes. Add more water if necessary to prevent sticking. Serve the sausages directly from the pan.

SUGGESTED ACCOMPANIMENT: *braised red cabbage.*

EDITOR'S NOTE: *Instead of sautéing, the sausages may be baked in a 375° F. oven for 30 to 40 minutes.*

Making Sausages

1 RINSING THE CASINGS. After soaking the casings, cut them into lengths of about 1 yard. Roll one end of each casing onto the spout of a funnel or tap, and run cold water through it; discard any casings that are punctured. Lay out the casings to drain.

2 FILLING A CASING. Secure a sausage-making attachment to a meat grinder or mixer. Roll a casing onto the nozzle; leave about 4 inches free and tie a knot in the end. Fill the bowl with the stuffing and turn the handle. As the casing fills, ease it off the nozzle.

3 FORMING LINKS. When only about 4 inches of the casing remains to be filled, slip it off the nozzle and knot it. Roll the casing on a work surface to even out the stuffing. To form links, twist the casing through three or four turns at intervals of about 6 inches.

Noisettes in Sherry-Vinegar Sauce

Serves 4
Working (and total) time: about 20 minutes

Calories **270**
Protein **24g.**
Cholesterol **70mg.**
Total fat **14g.**
Saturated fat **5g.**
Sodium **320mg.**

1 lb. pork tenderloin, trimmed of fat and cut into 16 slices
freshly ground black pepper
1 tbsp. virgin olive oil
10 garlic cloves, peeled
3 tbsp. sherry vinegar or red wine vinegar
1 tbsp. dry sherry
1½ lb. ripe tomatoes, peeled, seeded, and chopped, or 14 oz. canned whole tomatoes, drained
2 tbsp. unsalted chicken or veal stock (recipes, page 139)
1 tbsp. unsalted butter (optional)
¼ tsp. salt
¼ cup finely chopped parsley or chives for garnish

Rub the pork slices on both sides with some pepper. Heat the oil in a heavy-bottomed skillet over high heat, and when the oil is hot but not smoking, add the pork. Sear the pork on both sides and reduce the heat to very low. Add the garlic cloves. Continue cooking until the pork is firm but still springy to the touch—five to eight minutes, depending on the thickness of the pork. Remove the pork from the pan and keep it warm.

Increase the heat and deglaze the pan with the vinegar and sherry. Cook until almost all of the liquid has evaporated—about one minute. Add the tomatoes and stock, and cook over high heat until the mixture has reduced by half.

Remove the pan from the heat and sieve the mixture. Return the sauce and the meat to the pan, and reheat on low; if you wish, remove the pan from the heat and whisk in the butter to thicken the sauce.

Add the salt, arrange the pork on four plates, and spoon the sauce around it. Garnish with the chopped parsley or chives before serving.

SUGGESTED ACCOMPANIMENT: *green beans.*

Pork Patties with Eggplant Puree

Serves 4
Working (and total) time: about 30 minutes

Calories **220**
Protein **23g.**
Cholesterol **70mg.**
Total fat **12g.**
Saturated fat **4g.**
Sodium **120mg.**

1 lb. lean pork, trimmed of fat and ground or very finely chopped
2 scallions, white part only, finely chopped
2 tsp. ground coriander
one 1-lb. eggplant
1¼ tsp. cumin seeds
1 shallot, finely chopped
¼ cup plain low-fat yogurt
freshly ground black pepper
1 tbsp. safflower oil
cilantro sprigs for garnish (optional)

Mix the pork with the chopped scallions and the ground coriander, and form eight patties that are about 2½ inches in diameter.

Cut the eggplant in half lengthwise and place the halves in a vegetable steamer. Lay a sheet of wax paper over the top and steam the eggplant until tender—about 10 minutes.

Heat the cumin seeds in a nonstick frying pan over medium heat, stirring frequently, until they are fragrant and lightly toasted—about three minutes. Add the shallot, and cook until it is soft—about three minutes. Scoop the flesh from the eggplant, and puree it in a food processor or a blender with the cumin seeds and the shallots. Return the mixture to the frying pan, and stir in the low-fat yogurt and some freshly ground black pepper.

Heat the oil in another nonstick frying pan over high heat and brown the pork patties for about two minutes on each side, then reduce the heat and cook for another three minutes. Meanwhile, warm the puree over low heat, stirring constantly.

Spoon the puree onto four warmed plates. Place two patties on each plate and garnish with the sprigs of cilantro, if you are using them.

Porkburgers

Serves 4
Working (and total) time: about 35 minutes

Calories **340**
Protein **32g.**
Cholesterol **85mg.**
Total fat **12g.**
Saturated fat **4g.**
Sodium **550mg.**

½ lb. pork tenderloin, trimmed of fat and ground or very finely chopped
½ lb. veal round, trimmed of fat and ground or very finely chopped
1 onion, very finely chopped
¼ tsp. salt
½ tsp. dry mustard
¼ tsp. chili powder
1 tbsp. safflower oil
4 hamburger buns, split in half
4 crisp lettuce leaves, washed and dried
4 slices tomato
4 mild or hot pickled chili peppers
Chili topping
4 tbsp. chili relish
1 carrot, grated
2 shallots, finely chopped
1-inch piece cucumber, finely chopped

In a bowl, mix the pork with the veal, onion, salt, mustard, and chili powder. Form the mixture into four patties about ½ inch thick.

Heat the oil in a large frying pan over medium heat. Add the burgers and fry until brown and cooked through—about six minutes on each side.

Meanwhile, make the topping. In a bowl, mix the chili relish with the carrot, shallots, and cucumber. If you like, toast the buns under a broiler.

Arrange a lettuce leaf on the bottom portion of each bun, then add a burger to each, and top with a slice of tomato and a spoonful of chili topping. Cover with the bun tops and secure them in position with cocktail sticks. Garnish with the chilies and serve at once.

rice with moistened wax paper and keep it warm.

Heat the oil in a heavy-bottomed frying pan over low heat and cook the patties; turn them and gradually increase the heat so that they become crisp and brown all over. This should take about seven minutes. Remove the patties from the pan and keep them warm.

Over high heat, deglaze the pan with the balsamic vinegar. When it has all but disappeared, add 4 tablespoons of the reserved rice-cooking liquid or 4 tablespoons of stock or water, and reduce until it becomes syrupy. Add the remaining nutmeg and salt and some pepper. Serve the patties on warmed plates with the sauce around them and the rice to one side.

EDITOR'S NOTE: *For a richer sauce, add reduced chicken stock instead of the rice-cooking liquid to the deglazed pan.*

Prune and Pecan Patties

Serves 4
Working time: about 20 minutes
Total time: about 1 hour and 30 minutes

Calories **280**	½ lb. lean pork, ground or finely chopped
Protein **16g.**	1½ cups unsalted chicken stock (recipe, page 139) or water
Cholesterol **45mg.**	
Total fat **12g.**	½ cup wild rice, rinsed
Saturated fat **4g.**	8 prunes, pitted and soaked in 1 tbsp. dry Madeira for one hour
Sodium **150mg.**	
	⅓ cup pecans
	1½ tsp. grated nutmeg
	¼ tsp. salt
	1 tbsp. safflower oil
	3 tbsp. balsamic vinegar, or 3 tbsp. red wine vinegar, plus 1 tbsp. honey
	freshly ground black pepper

In a saucepan, bring 1¼ cups of the stock or water to a boil, and add the wild rice. Cook the rice, covered, for about one hour, checking it periodically and adding more stock or water if necessary. Meanwhile, chop the prunes and pecans finely, and combine them with the pork, ½ teaspoon of the nutmeg, and half of the salt. Shape the mixture into eight patties with your hands.

When the rice is cooked—the grains should be split open and soft but still have some bite—drain it and reserve the cooking liquid, if there is any left. Cover the

Watercress Pork

Serves 4
Working (and total) time: about 25 minutes

Calories **195**	1 lb. pork tenderloin, trimmed of fat and cut into 3-by-¾-inch strips
Protein **25g.**	
Cholesterol **70mg.**	1 bunch watercress, leaves and fine stems only
Total fat **10g.**	1 cup unsalted chicken or veal stock (recipes, page 139)
Saturated fat **5g.**	
Sodium **275mg.**	1 shallot, finely chopped
	3 tbsp. dry white wine
	⅓ cup plain low-fat yogurt
	¼ tsp. salt
	freshly ground black pepper

Reserve some of the watercress for a garnish; bring the stock to a boil and blanch the remaining watercress for one minute. Drain, reserving the stock, then refresh the watercress under cold running water. Drain the watercress again, then place it on paper towels to dry.

In a nonstick skillet over medium-high heat, cook the pork for two to three minutes, turning the strips so they become an even light brown on the outside and are just cooked in the center. Transfer the strips to a warmed plate using a slotted spoon, and cover the strips to keep them warm. Lower the heat beneath the pan, add the shallot and wine, and cook, stirring occasionally, until the shallots are soft and the wine is almost completely evaporated—about three minutes. Add the reserved stock, increase the heat, and reduce the liquid until there are only about 3 tablespoons left; add any juices from the pork a few minutes before the end of cooking. In a food processor or a blender, puree the watercress with the reduced stock. Blend in the yogurt; add the salt and some pepper.

In a pan, reheat the sauce on low, stirring; just before serving, add the pork and fold through to coat the strips. Garnish with the reserved watercress.

SUGGESTED ACCOMPANIMENT: *couscous or noodles.*

Pepper Pork with Mozzarella

Serves 4
Working time: about 25 minutes
Total time: about 40 minutes

Calories **240**
Protein **25g.**
Cholesterol **90mg.**
Total fat **14g.**
Saturated fat **5g.**
Sodium **225mg.**

1 lb. pork tenderloin, trimmed of fat
1 tsp. black peppercorns
1 tsp. green peppercorns in brine, rinsed, drained, and chopped
1 tbsp. safflower oil
1 garlic clove, halved
½ cup grated part-skim mozzarella
2 shallots, finely chopped
hot red-pepper sauce
Worcestershire sauce
⅔ cup unsalted chicken stock (recipe, page 139)
2 tbsp. dry sherry
4 sprigs flat-leaf parsley

Lay the pork on a board, and with a knife, cut it at a slightly diagonal angle into 12 slices, each about ¾ inch thick. Crush the black peppercorns using a pestle and mortar. Sprinkle the black and green pepper over one side of the pork slices, and press it into the meat. Cover the slices and set them aside for 15 minutes.

Heat the oil in a heavy-bottomed or nonstick frying pan on medium. Add the garlic and pork, peppered side down, and cook until well browned—about three minutes on each side. Preheat the broiler. Remove the pork from the pan and arrange the slices, peppered side up, in two overlapping rows in a shallow, flame-proof dish. Sprinkle the mozzarella over the pork, and broil until the cheese has melted and begins to brown.

Meanwhile, remove the garlic from the pan and discard it. Add the shallots to the pan and stir well, scraping up any browned bits from the bottom of the pan. Stir in a few drops each of hot red-pepper sauce and Worcestershire sauce, and add the stock and sherry. Simmer the sauce until it is slightly reduced—about three minutes. Spoon the sauce around the pork steaks and serve at once, garnished with the parsley.

SUGGESTED ACCOMPANIMENTS: *new potatoes; green salad.*

Cutlets with Tomato and Mozzarella

Serves 4
Working time: about 20 minutes
Total time: about 40 minutes

Calories **295**
Protein **25g.**
Cholesterol **70mg.**
Total fat **18g.**
Saturated fat **6g.**
Sodium **290mg.**

4 pork cutlets, trimmed of fat (about 4 oz. each)
2 tbsp. virgin olive oil
1 small onion, finely chopped
1 small carrot, finely chopped
½ celery stalk, finely chopped
1½ lb. ripe tomatoes, peeled and seeded, or 14 oz. canned tomatoes, drained
1 tbsp. tomato paste
2 bay leaves
freshly ground black pepper
1 cup chopped fresh basil
2½ oz. part-skim mozzarella, thinly sliced

Heat 1 tablespoon of the oil in a heavy-bottomed or nonstick saucepan, and cook the onion, carrot, and celery over low heat until they are soft—about three minutes. Add the tomatoes, tomato paste, and the bay leaves to the pan, and cook for 20 minutes, or until the sauce is no longer runny, stirring frequently.

Preheat the broiler. Season the cutlets with some pepper, rubbing it in with your fingertips. In a heavy-bottomed or nonstick frying pan, heat the remaining oil over high heat until it is hot but not smoking, and cook the pork until it is brown on both sides—about two minutes. Remove the pan from the heat and allow the meat to sizzle for two minutes, turning once.

Transfer the cutlets to a broiling pan and spread equal portions of the tomato sauce over them, then sprinkle with the basil and top with the mozzarella. Heat under the broiler for one minute, or until the cheese has melted. Serve immediately.

SUGGESTED ACCOMPANIMENTS: *boiled rice; green salad.*

Pork with a Passion-Fruit Sauce

Serves 4
Working time: about 15 minutes
Total time: about 3 hours and 15 minutes
(includes marinating)

Calories **260**
Protein **32g.**
Cholesterol **70mg.**
Total fat **11g.**
Saturated fat **4g.**
Sodium **110mg.**

4 pork loin chops (4½ to 5 oz. each), trimmed of fat
4 passion fruit
¾ cup dry white wine
1 tsp. sugar (optional)
ground white pepper

Pound the steaks with a mallet to flatten them slightly *(page 12, Step 2)*, then place them in a single layer in a shallow, nonreactive dish.

Squeeze the juice from the passion fruit; reserve the seeds. Pour the juice onto the pork and spread the seeds over its surface. Cover the dish and set it aside to marinate in a cool place for three hours, turning the pork frequently.

Preheat the broiler. Remove the pork from the marinade and brush off any seeds adhering to it; reserve the marinade. Place the steaks close to the source of heat and broil until lightly charred on the surface but still tender in the center—about four minutes on each side. Meanwhile, in a small saucepan, boil the wine until it is reduced to about ¼ cup, then stir in the reserved marinade and heat it through. Add the sugar if desired; season with some white pepper.

Serve the pork with the sauce spooned over it.

EDITOR'S NOTE: *If you prefer, the passion-fruit juice may be strained and the seeds discarded.*

Chilies—A Cautionary Note

Both dried and fresh hot chilies should be handled with care. Their flesh and seeds contain volatile oils that can make skin tingle and cause eyes to burn. Rubber gloves offer protection—but the cook should still be careful not to touch the face, lips, or eyes when working with chilies.

Soaking fresh chilies in cold, salted water for an hour will remove some of their fire. If canned chilies are substituted for fresh ones, they should be rinsed in cold water in order to eliminate as much of the brine used to preserve them as possible.

Indian Chops

Serves 4
Working time: about 25 minutes
Total time: about 1 day (includes marinating)

Calories **290**
Protein **40g.**
Cholesterol **70mg.**
Total fat **14g.**
Saturated fat **5g.**
Sodium **225mg.**

4 pork chops (about 4½ to 5 oz. each), trimmed of fat	
1 fresh chili pepper or 1 dried chili pepper soaked in water for 30 minutes, seeded and chopped (caution, box, opposite)	
1 small piece turmeric stem, or ½ tsp. dry mustard	
2 garlic cloves	
½ tsp. fenugreek seeds (optional)	
½ tsp. coriander seeds	
½ tsp. cumin seeds	
½ tsp. salt	
4 tbsp. plain low-fat yogurt	

Using a mortar and pestle, pound the chili pepper and the turmeric or mustard powder, the garlic cloves, the fenugreek seeds, if you are using them, the coriander seeds and the cumin seeds, and the salt into a coarse paste. Stir the yogurt into the paste and mix well.

Coat the pork chops with the yogurt mixture, place them in a nonreactive dish, cover with plastic wrap, and let them marinate in the refrigerator for 24 hours.

Preheat the broiler. Remove the chops from the marinade, wipe them with paper towels, and brush off any dry ingredients that are sticking to them. Heat one or two metal skewers over high heat on the stove, and print a crisscross pattern on both sides of each chop by pressing the skewer gently onto the surface.

Broil the chops until cooked through—about six minutes on each side. Set the chops aside in a warm place to rest for five minutes before serving.

SUGGESTED ACCOMPANIMENTS: *new potatoes with toasted poppy seeds; cucumber in a yogurt and mint dressing.*

EDITOR'S NOTE: *Ground spices may be substituted for the turmeric stem and the fenugreek, coriander, and cumin seeds, but grinding the ingredients in a mortar yields a better flavor. If you barbecue the chops on a grill over coals, you do not need to sear them with a skewer.*

Pork Chops with Kumquats

Serves 4
Working time: about 20 minutes
Total time: about 2 hours and 20 minutes
(includes marinating)

Calories **320**
Protein **33g.**
Cholesterol **80mg.**
Total fat **13g.**
Saturated fat **6g.**
Sodium **280mg.**

4 pork chops, trimmed of fat (4½ to 5 oz. each)
⅓ cup dry white wine or vermouth
⅓ cup fresh orange juice
2 tsp. honey
1½ cups ripe kumquats
½ tsp. salt
freshly ground black pepper
1 tbsp. unsalted butter, chilled

Combine the wine or vermouth with the orange juice and honey in a nonreactive dish. Add the pork and let it marinate for at least two hours. Remove the meat from the dish and reserve the marinade. Dry the meat with paper towels and set it aside. Preheat the broiler.

Reserve four of the kumquats for a garnish; puree the remainder in a food processor with the reserved marinade, then pass the puree through a fine sieve. The kumquat skins and seeds will be left behind. In a saucepan over high heat, bring the puree to a boil and reduce it for about one minute, or until it is thick and bright orange. Remove the pan from the heat.

Season the pork with the salt and some pepper, and broil until cooked through—about six minutes on each side. Reheat the sauce, then remove the pan from the heat and whisk in the chilled butter. Serve the chops with the sauce spooned around them, garnished with slices of the reserved kumquats.

Chops with Mustard and Dill Sauce

Serves 6
Working (and total) time: about 25 minutes

Calories **260**
Protein **34g.**
Cholesterol **80mg.**
Total fat **17g.**
Saturated fat **7g.**
Sodium **350mg.**

6 pork chops, trimmed of fat (4½ to 5 oz. each)
3 tbsp. red peppercorns
1 cup plain low-fat yogurt
1 tbsp. prepared English mustard or other mustard
1½ tbsp. chopped dill
½ tsp. salt

Preheat the broiler. Crush the peppercorns in a mortar and press them onto both sides of the chops. To make the sauce, mix together the yogurt, mustard, dill, and salt. Refrigerate the sauce while you cook the chops.

Broil the chops until the juices run clear when the meat is pricked with a skewer—about six minutes on each side. Serve the chops immediately with the mustard and dill sauce.

EDITOR'S NOTE: *If red peppercorns are not available, crush a few juniper berries with some black peppercorns.*

Kabobs with Red Peppers and Grapefruit

Serves 6
Working time: about 20 minutes
Total time: about 1 hour and 15 minutes (includes marinating)

Calories **225**
Protein **22g.**
Cholesterol **70mg.**
Total fat **12g.**
Saturated fat **3g.**
Sodium **145mg.**

1½ lb. pork tenderloin, trimmed of fat and cut into about 36 cubes
4 tbsp. safflower oil
1 tbsp. wine vinegar
2 tbsp. finely cut chives
¼ tsp. salt
freshly ground black pepper
3 grapefruit
2 or 3 sweet red peppers

Mix together the oil, vinegar, and chives, add the salt and some pepper, and marinate the meat in this mix-ture for about one hour. While the meat marinates, slice off all the peel from the grapefruit and cut out the segments of flesh. Seed and derib the peppers, and cut them into 1-inch squares.

Remove the meat from the marinade, and thread the cubes onto 12 small skewers, alternating one pep-per square and one grapefruit segment between each cube of pork. Preheat the broiler and cook the kabobs for about 10 minutes, turning once—take care when turning the skewers not to break the grapefruit seg-ments. Do not overcook: The meat should be moist and the peppers still firm.

Serve the kabobs immediately.

SUGGESTED ACCOMPANIMENTS: *plain boiled rice; green salad.*

EDITOR'S NOTE: *If you use wooden skewers, soak them in water for about 10 minutes before threading them with the pork—this will prevent them from burning under the broiler.*

Kabobs in Tea and Ginger Marinade

Serves 4
Working time: about 35 minutes
Total time: about 9 hours (includes marinating)

Calories **160**
Protein **22g.**
Cholesterol **70mg.**
Total fat **8g.**
Saturated fat **3g.**
Sodium **80mg.**

1 lb. pork tenderloin, trimmed of fat and cut into 24 cubes	
16 shallots, peeled, or 16 scallion bulbs	
16 button mushrooms	

Tea marinade

1 tsp. Earl Grey tea leaves
1 garlic clove, crushed
2 tbsp. finely chopped fresh ginger
4 tbsp. dry sherry
1 tbsp. light brown sugar
2 tbsp. virgin olive oil

To make the marinade, put the tea leaves into a cup and pour ½ cup of boiling water over the leaves. Let them steep for four minutes, then strain the tea into a medium-size bowl. Add the garlic clove, ginger, sherry, brown sugar, and oil to the bowl, and mix well.

Add the pork cubes to the bowl and turn them to coat them with the marinade. Cover the bowl and set it in the refrigerator for eight hours, or overnight.

Preheat the broiler. Drain the meat, reserving the marinade. Thread the pork, alternating with the shallots and mushrooms, onto eight skewers. Brush the kabobs with the marinade and broil, about 5 inches from the heat, for 15 minutes, turning and basting them frequently with the marinade. Serve hot.

SUGGESTED ACCOMPANIMENT: *pureed turnips.*

EDITOR'S NOTE: *Soak wooden skewers for about 10 minutes before threading them to keep them from burning.*

Nordic Cutlets

Serves 4
Working time: about 20 minutes
Total time: about 50 minutes (includes marinating)

Calories **220**
Protein **22g.**
Cholesterol **70mg.**
Total fat **12g.**
Saturated fat **3g.**
Sodium **280mg.**

1 lb. pork tenderloin, trimmed of fat
½ cup dry white wine
1 tbsp. safflower oil
3 tbsp. finely chopped dill
1 large cucumber
½ tsp. salt
freshly ground black pepper
½ cup finely chopped dill pickles
¼ cup plain low-fat yogurt

Slice the tenderloin diagonally into eight cutlets, then pound the cutlets until they are about ¼ inch thick *(technique, page 12)*. Put the cutlets into a nonreactive bowl with the wine, oil, and 2 tablespoons of the chopped dill. Marinate them for at least 30 minutes.

Toward the end of this time, peel the cucumber and cut it in half lengthwise. Using a teaspoon, scrape out the seeds and discard them. Finely dice the flesh of the cucumber and transfer it to a saucepan.

Remove the meat from the marinade and shake off any excess liquid. Pour the marinade over the cucumber, add ¼ teaspoon of the salt and some pepper, then bring the mixture to a boil. Cover and cook over medium heat for five minutes; then remove the lid, and stirring all the time, cook until most of the liquid has evaporated and the cucumber is quite dry. While the cucumber is cooking, stir the pickles into the pan with the remaining dill. Remove the pan from the heat.

Preheat the broiler. Sprinkle the cutlets with the remaining salt and some pepper, then sear them until flecked with brown—about two minutes on each side.

Reheat the cucumber on low and stir in the yogurt—do not allow the mixture to boil. Serve two cutlets on each plate, with the cucumber spooned around them.

SUGGESTED ACCOMPANIMENT: *boiled new potatoes.*

Deviled Medallions

Serves 4
Working time: about 25 minutes
Total time: about 35 minutes

Calories **275**
Protein **25g.**
Cholesterol **70mg.**
Total fat **8g.**
Saturated fat **3g.**
Sodium **320mg.**

1 lb. boned pork loin, trimmed of fat and cut into eight medallions about ½ inch thick
2 tbsp. Dijon mustard
3 tbsp. dry white wine
½ tsp. hot paprika, or ½ tsp. paprika mixed with ⅛ tsp. cayenne pepper
freshly ground black pepper
1½ cups fine dry whole-wheat bread crumbs

Peach chutney

2 ripe peaches (about ½ lb.)
1 tbsp. capers, rinsed and chopped
1 or 2 scallions, finely chopped
1 tbsp. fresh lemon juice

First, make the chutney. Peel and pit both peaches, then puree one peach in a blender or a food processor, and pour the puree into a bowl. Coarsely chop the other peach, and stir it into the puree along with the capers, scallions, and lemon juice. Set aside.

Combine the mustard, wine, paprika, and some black pepper in a shallow dish. Stir the mixture until it is smooth. Spread the bread crumbs on a plate or a sheet of wax paper. Dip the medallions, one at a time, in the mustard mixture and gently shake off the excess; then coat both sides and around the edges with the crumbs, pressing them on so they adhere. Let the medallions dry briefly. Meanwhile, preheat the broiler.

Broil the medallions about 5 inches from the heat source until they are lightly browned and cooked through—about five minutes on each side.

Arrange the medallions on a warm platter or individual plates. Serve with the chutney.

Pork Char-Shiu

CHAR-SHIU—IN CANTONESE, "ROASTED ON A FORK"—IS THE
NAME OF A CHINESE CHARCOAL-GRILLED PORK DISH. IN
THIS VERSION, ALL FAT IS TRIMMED OFF THE MEAT AND A LIGHT
GLAZING SYRUP KEEPS THE MEAT MOIST DURING
COOKING; IT CAN BE COOKED AT HOME UNDER A BROILER OR,
BETTER STILL, ON A BARBECUE.

Serves 4
Working time: about 30 minutes
Total time: about 3 hours and 30 minutes
(includes marinating)

Calories **230**
Protein **27g.**
Cholesterol **90mg.**
Total fat **9g.**
Saturated fat **4g.**
Sodium **100mg.**

2 pork tenderloins (about ¾ lb. each), thin ends cut off, trimmed of fat
2 tbsp. low-sodium soy sauce
3 or 4 scallions, finely chopped
1-inch piece fresh ginger, finely chopped
2 garlic cloves, finely chopped
½ tsp. Sichuan pepper
2 star anise
1 tbsp. dry sherry
1 tbsp. honey
1½ tsp. red wine vinegar
½ tsp. cornstarch, mixed with 2 tbsp. water
mixed salad leaves, washed and dried

Rub the pork with 1 tablespoon of the soy sauce and
set it aside for 20 minutes at room temperature. In a
mortar, pound the scallions, ginger, and garlic to a
coarse paste with the Sichuan pepper and star anise.
Mix in the sherry, the remaining soy sauce, half of the
honey, and 1 teaspoon of the vinegar; coat the pork
with the paste and let it marinate for two to six hours
in the refrigerator, turning it once or twice.

Remove the pork from the refrigerator, pat it dry
with paper towels, and remove any scallions, ginger,
or garlic that is sticking to it. Strain the marinade into
a small, nonreactive saucepan and reserve it. Prepare
a glazing syrup by mixing 1 teaspoon of hot water with
the remaining honey and vinegar.

Preheat the broiler, place the meat several inches
from the source of heat, and cook it on both sides until

brown—about four minutes per side. Move the meat to about 4 inches from the heat source and cook for another 10 minutes, turning the meat a few times and basting it with the glazing syrup. Test for doneness with a skewer—the juice that runs out should be almost clear. Cover the cooked tenderloin loosely with aluminum foil and let it rest for five minutes.

Bring the reserved marinade to a simmer, add the cornstarch mixture, and cook, stirring, until the mixture thickens—one to two minutes. To serve, slice the tenderloins into thin rounds and place them on a bed of salad leaves. Serve the heated marinade separately as a dipping sauce.

SUGGESTED ACCOMPANIMENT: *plain boiled rice or stir-fried mixed vegetables.*

Pork Kofta

COMMON IN INDIAN AND MIDDLE EASTERN COOKING, KOFTA IS SEASONED GROUND MEAT SHAPED INTO BALLS OR SAUSAGES.

Serves 4
Working time: about 35 minutes
Total time: about 2 hours and 30 minutes
(includes marinating)

Calories **375**
Protein **30g.**
Cholesterol **80mg.**
Total fat **20g.**
Saturated fat **5g.**
Sodium **510mg.**

1 lb. pork tenderloin, ground or very finely chopped
1 lemon, grated zest only
2 garlic cloves, crushed
1 tbsp. coriander seeds, toasted and coarsely ground
½ tsp. salt
freshly ground black pepper
3 tbsp. dry white wine
1½ tbsp. fresh lemon juice
1½ tbsp. virgin olive oil
4 carrots, grated
1 cup chopped cilantro
4 pita breads

Combine the ground pork, lemon zest, garlic, coriander seeds, salt, and some pepper. Divide the mixture into four parts, and roll each part into a sausage shape about 6 inches long and 1 inch thick.

Place the kofta in a shallow dish, and add the wine, 1 tablespoon of the lemon juice, and the oil. Marinate the kofta for two hours, turning them frequently.

Preheat the broiler. Mix the grated carrots with the cilantro and the remaining lemon juice.

Remove the kofta from the marinade, and broil on high until the pork is firm and well browned on all sides—about seven minutes. While the kofta cooks, warm the pita bread in a 325° F. oven.

To serve, slit open one side of each warm pita bread to make a pocket. Fill each pocket with one-quarter of the carrot and cilantro salad and a kofta.

SUGGESTED ACCOMPANIMENT: *yogurt, to be spooned into the pita breads according to taste.*

Citrus Satay

Serves 4
Working (and total) time: about 45 minutes

Calories **220**
Protein **24g.**
Cholesterol **85mg.**
Total fat **12g.**
Saturated fat **4g.**
Sodium **400mg.**

¾ lb. lean ground or very finely chopped pork
¼ lb. shrimp, peeled and deveined
1 garlic clove
½-inch piece fresh ginger
½ tsp. fresh lime juice
½ tsp. arrowroot
¾ tsp. salt
2 tbsp. chopped cilantro
¼ tsp. ground dried lemon peel (optional)
¼ tsp. tamarind concentrate (optional)
2 tsp. safflower oil
Peanut-yogurt satay sauce
⅓ cup dry roasted peanuts without added salt
½ tsp. grated lime zest, plus 1 tsp. fresh lime juice
½ tsp. dark brown sugar
1½ tsp. low-sodium soy sauce
⅛ tsp. salt
4 tbsp. plain low-fat yogurt
⅛ tsp. chili powder

In a mortar, pound the shrimp with the garlic, ginger, lime juice, and arrowroot. Alternatively, chop the garlic and ginger in a food processor, add the shrimp, lime juice, and arrowroot, and process until a paste is formed—about 15 seconds. Chill the mixture to make it easier to handle. Combine the pork with the salt, cilantro, and the lemon peel and tamarind, if you are using them. Form the mixture into eight flat, oval patties. Spoon one-eighth of the shrimp mixture onto each patty; mold the pork around the filling to enclose it. Chill the meat if you are not cooking it immediately.

Preheat the broiler. Insert a wooden satay stick or a metal skewer lengthwise through each portion of meat; alternatively, cook and serve the meat without the sticks. Brush a broiling pan with a little of the oil, place the meat in the pan, and brush the top with a little more oil. Broil the meat until, turning it once, it is brown on both sides—about 10 minutes. Meanwhile, make the sauce. Grind the nuts in a food processor; add the lime zest and juice, sugar, soy sauce, and salt. Beat in the yogurt and add the chili powder. Serve the sauce in a bowl to accompany the satays.

SUGGESTED ACCOMPANIMENTS: *citrus rice; a crisp salad.*

EDITOR'S NOTE: *The sauce may be prepared in advance but will thicken a little on standing. If you are using wooden skewers, soak them in water for about 20 minutes before threading them with the meat—this will prevent them from burning.*

Mediterranean Kidneys

KIDNEYS ARE A RICH SOURCE OF VITAMINS BUT HAVE A RELATIVELY HIGH CHOLESTEROL CONTENT, WHICH SHOULD BE TAKEN INTO ACCOUNT WHEN PLANNING THE REST OF THE DAY'S MENU.

Serves 4
Working (and total) time: about 50 minutes

Calories **180**
Protein **8g.**
Cholesterol **360mg.**
Total fat **12g.**
Saturated fat **5g.**
Sodium **510mg.**

| 4 pork kidneys (about 4 oz. each), trimmed of fat |
| 1 tbsp. virgin olive oil |
| 1 garlic clove, finely chopped |
| ½ lb. fennel, roughly chopped, feathery tops reserved for garnish |
| ½ lb. ripe tomatoes, peeled, seeded, and chopped |
| 1 tbsp. fresh lemon juice |
| 2 tbsp. chopped basil or oregano |
| ½ tsp. salt |
| freshly ground black pepper |
| 2 tbsp. unsalted butter, chilled |

Heat ½ tablespoon of the oil in a heavy-bottomed pan over low heat. Add the garlic, fennel, tomatoes, and lemon juice, cover, and cook until the fennel is tender—about 30 minutes. Remove the lid and increase the heat; stirring all the time, boil off any liquid and cook the vegetables until they are just beginning to stick to the bottom of the pan. Stir in the basil or oregano, half of the salt, and some pepper. Briefly puree the vegetables in a food processor, or pass them through a sieve. Return the puree to the pan.

Peel off the fat and membrane from the kidneys, and cut out the white cores (technique, below). Preheat the broiler. Thread two thin parallel, short skewers through each kidney so that the kidneys will stay flat while cooking. Brush all surfaces of the kidneys with the remaining oil, and season them with the remaining salt and some more black pepper.

Broil the kidneys for about three minutes on each side, so that the surfaces are well colored but the insides are still pink. Remove the skewers; arrange the kidneys on a serving plate and keep them warm.

Cut the butter into tiny cubes, and beat them into the fennel puree over low heat to make the sauce glossy. Spoon the puree over the kidneys, garnish with the reserved fennel tops, and serve immediately.

SUGGESTED ACCOMPANIMENT: salad with mustard vinaigrette.

EDITOR'S NOTE: If you use wooden skewers, soak them in water for about 10 minutes before threading them with the kidneys—this will prevent them from burning.

Preparing a Kidney

1 PEELING OFF THE MEMBRANE. With a sharp knife, make a shallow slit in the rounded side of the kidney to pierce the translucent membrane that encloses it. Peel off the membrane and sever it from the core at the concave side of the kidney.

2 OPENING THE KIDNEY. Make a lengthwise cut into the kidney's rounded side until you feel the strands of core inside the kidney resisting the blade. Fold back the upper section, then cut through the strands and deepen the cut to within ¼ inch of the concave side.

3 CUTTING OUT THE CORE. With the kidney laid open on the work surface, use a pair of scissors to snip out the white core. Take care not to separate the two halves of the kidney.

Prune Tenderloin Wrapped in Grape Leaves

Serves 6
Working time: about 30 minutes
Total time: about 5 hours (includes soaking)

Calories **280**
Protein **33g.**
Cholesterol **70mg.**
Total fat **11g.**
Saturated fat **4g.**
Sodium **100mg.**

2 pork tenderloins (about ¾ lb. each), trimmed of fat
18 prunes, soaked for 4 hours in 1½ tbsp. brandy and boiling water to cover
½ tsp. salt
freshly ground black pepper
18 juniper berries
about 15 fresh grape leaves
5 tbsp. unsalted chicken stock (recipe, page 139)

Remove the prunes from their soaking liquid when they are soft, and pit them; reserve the soaking liquid. Preheat the oven to 450° F.

Cut a lengthwise incision in each tenderloin and pound the tenderloins gently with a wooden mallet to flatten them *(technique, page 11)*. Season the meat lightly with the salt and some pepper.

With the cut side of the tenderloins facing up, place the prunes and juniper berries in the center of the tenderloins, and fold the meat around them to make two long, thin rolls. Wrap the rolls with some of the grape leaves and tie them with string in several places. Put the wrapped rolls in a roasting pan with the stock, cover with foil, and cook in the oven for 30 minutes.

Take the meat out of the oven, remove it from the pan, and let it rest for 10 to 15 minutes. Add the reserved prune-soaking liquid to the juices in the pan and boil for one minute on medium, scraping up the browned bits on the bottom of the pan with a spoon.

Arrange the remaining grape leaves on a warm serving dish. Slice the tenderloins and remove the string. Place the slices in the middle of the dish and pour the cooking juices over them.

EDITOR'S NOTE: *If you are using preserved grape leaves, blanch them in boiling water for two to three minutes to remove the salt, and rinse well. The grape leaves arranged on the serving dish will soak up some of the cooking juices and can be eaten.*

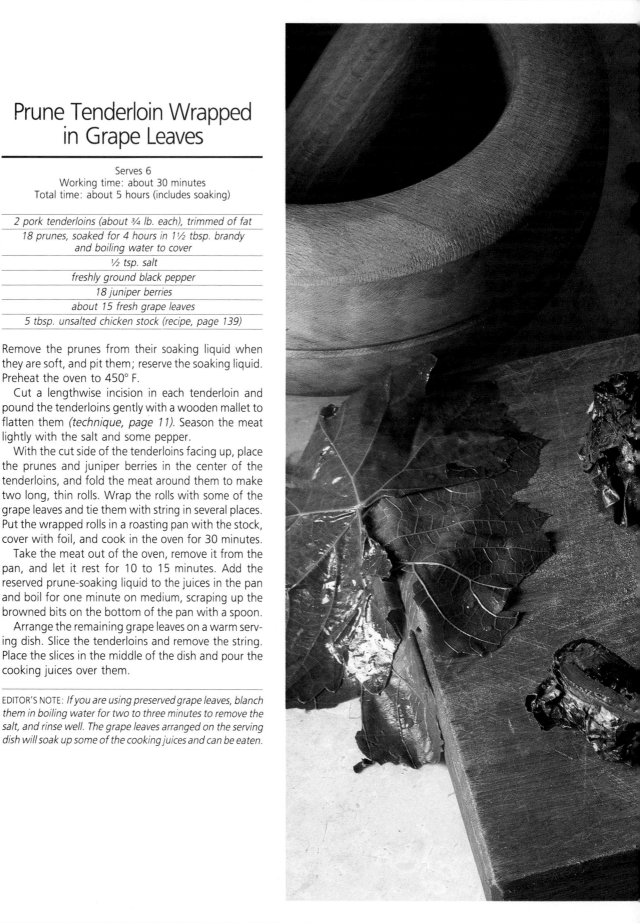

Fava Bean Pork

Serves 4
Working time: about 30 minutes
Total time: about 1 hour and 20 minutes

Calories **280**
Protein **33g.**
Cholesterol **70mg.**
Total fat **14g.**
Saturated fat **4g.**
Sodium **125mg.**

1 lb. boned pork loin, trimmed of fat
freshly ground black pepper
1 cup cooked shelled young fava beans
1 tbsp. plain low-fat yogurt
1 tsp. chopped fresh summer savory
1 tsp. fresh lemon juice
⅓ cup dry white wine
¾ cup unsalted chicken stock (recipe, page 139)

Preheat the oven to 350° F.

If the pork loin has been rolled and tied by the butcher, first untie and unroll it, then season the inside surface of the loin with a few generous grindings of black pepper.

Puree the fava beans with the yogurt in a food processor, then pass the puree through a nonmetallic sieve. Stir in the summer savory, add the lemon juice, and spread the mixture over the inside surface of the boned loin. Roll the pork up, lay a strip of foil over the exposed stuffing, and tie it into shape with string.

Heat a heavy roasting pan or a flameproof casserole, add the pork, and cook over medium-high heat, turning the pork so that it browns evenly—about five minutes. Then cook in the oven until the pork is done—about 50 minutes.

Transfer the pork to a warmed serving platter, cover it loosely, and let it rest in a warm place. Pour the wine into the roasting pan and boil, stirring frequently, until the wine is almost completely evaporated. Stir in the stock and boil again until it is very slightly thickened. Add freshly ground black pepper and a little more lemon juice, if you wish.

Carve the pork into slices and spoon the sauce around each serving.

SUGGESTED ACCOMPANIMENT: *green noodles.*

EDITOR'S NOTE: *A boned pork loin may also be stuffed with the spinach and mushroom mixture enclosed in a tenderloin in the recipe on page 52. For a 1-pound loin, use half the amount of stuffing required for the tenderloin.*

Pot-Roasted Pork Loin with Cherry Tomatoes

Serves 6
Working time: about 20 minutes
Total time: about 1 hour and 20 minutes

Calories **260**
Protein **30g.**
Cholesterol **70mg.**
Total fat **13g.**
Saturated fat **4g.**
Sodium **90mg.**

1½ lb. boned pork loin, trimmed of fat
1 tbsp. virgin olive oil
2 tsp. fennel seeds
1 tsp. green peppercorns
2 tbsp. white wine vinegar
2 tbsp. white wine
¼ tsp. salt
½ lb. cherry tomatoes, peeled

Heat the oil in a flameproof casserole that is just large enough to hold the pork loin, then, over medium heat, lightly brown the meat all over—about six minutes. Pour off and discard the oil, and add the fennel seeds, peppercorns, vinegar, wine, and salt to the casserole. Cover and cook over low heat for one hour; check the level of the liquid occasionally, and add more vinegar and wine if necessary. About 10 minutes before the end of cooking, add the tomatoes to the casserole.

Carefully remove the meat from the casserole and cut it into ¼-inch-thick slices. Overlap the slices in the middle of a warmed serving dish and arrange the tomatoes along the edges of the dish. Skim the fat from the surface of the liquid in the casserole, then pour the juices over the meat, making sure to include the fennel seeds and peppercorns.

Tenderloin with Spinach, Porcini, and Chestnuts

THIS DISH IS INTENDED TO BE SERVED COLD.

Serves 6
Working time: about 30 minutes
Total time: about 1 hour and 10 minutes

Calories **190**
Protein **24g.**
Cholesterol **70mg.**
Total fat **8g.**
Saturated fat **3g.**
Sodium **270mg.**

¾ lb. pork tenderloin in one piece
½ lb. pork tenderloin, ground or very finely chopped (technique, page 11)
1 lb. fresh spinach, washed and stemmed
½ tsp. coriander seeds
1 tsp. yellow mustard seeds
¼ tsp. ground mace
½ tsp. salt
freshly ground black pepper
2 oz. fresh porcini, or ⅓ oz. dried porcini, soaked for 20 minutes in hot water
½ cup peeled fresh chestnuts
1 tsp. safflower oil

Trim the pork of all visible fat, sinew, and transparent skin; wipe it clean. Slit the tenderloin lengthwise with a sharp knife to a depth of half its thickness, and flatten it out by pounding it firmly (technique, page 11).

Steam the spinach briefly in the water still clinging to its leaves after washing; refresh it under cold running water, squeeze hard to extract all moisture, and chop it finely. Lightly toast the coriander and mustard seeds. Crush the coriander seeds in a mortar, and combine them with the mustard seeds, mace, salt, and some pepper. If you are using dried mushrooms, strain and pat them dry. Mix the ground or very finely chopped pork with the spinach and the crushed spices. Spread this mixture over the flattened-out tenderloin, and arrange the mushrooms and the chestnuts along its length. Close up the tenderloin and use string to tie around the circumference in about six places.

Preheat the oven to 375° F. Heat the oil in a large, nonstick frying pan over medium-high heat, and place the tenderloin in the pan seam side down. Cook the tenderloin, turning it several times, until it is brown all over—five to 10 minutes. Wrap the tenderloin in aluminum foil and transfer it to a roasting pan. Cook the tenderloin in the oven for 40 minutes.

Allow the meat to cool in the foil, then refrigerate it. To serve, cut two or three slices for each person.

SUGGESTED ACCOMPANIMENT: red-leaf salad (such as oak-leaf lettuce or radicchio) or spinach.

Roast Pork Tenderloin with Pineapple Coulis

Serves 6
Working time: about 30 minutes
Total time: about 50 minutes

Calories **165**
Protein **20g.**
Cholesterol **70mg.**
Total fat **7g.**
Saturated fat **3g.**
Sodium **140mg.**

1½ lb. pork tenderloin, trimmed of fat
¼ tsp. salt
freshly ground black pepper
1 pineapple
1 tbsp. finely chopped cilantro or parsley leaves

Preheat the oven to 350° F.

Season the tenderloin with the salt and some pep-per, then wrap it in lightly greased foil and place it in a roasting pan. Cook the tenderloin in the oven for 35 to 45 minutes, or until the juices run clear.

While the meat cooks, peel and core the pineapple. Puree the fruit in a food processor or a blender, then pass it through a sieve. Refrigerate the coulis until you are ready to use it.

When the meat is cooked, unwrap it and add about a tablespoon of the juices collected in the foil to the pineapple coulis. Carve the meat into slices. Spread one or two spoonfuls of coulis on each serving plate, and arrange the slices of meat around it. Sprinkle with the cilantro or parsley.

Grape Pork

Serves 8
Working time: about 45 minutes
Total time: about 2 hours and 15 minutes

Calories **245**
Protein **22g.**
Cholesterol **80mg.**
Total fat **8g.**
Saturated fat **2g.**
Sodium **252mg.**

2 lb. boned leg of pork, rump end, trimmed of fat
1½ lb. green grapes, halved and seeded, or 1½ lb. small seedless green grapes
1 tsp. virgin olive oil
½ onion, finely chopped
1 small garlic clove, crushed
1½ cups fine fresh bread crumbs
¼ tsp. ground allspice
2 tsp. Worcestershire sauce
½ beaten egg
¾ tsp. salt
freshly ground black pepper
1 tbsp. arrowroot
½ cup dry Madeira

Preheat the oven to 350° F. Lay out the pork on a work surface with its inner side facing up and cut five or six lengthwise slits in it about 1½ inches deep, at equal intervals. Put 1 pound of the grapes into a food processor and blend to a smooth puree; sieve the puree over a bowl to strain the juice.

Heat the oil in a small, nonstick skillet, and add the onion, garlic, and 2 tablespoons of the grape juice. Cook the mixture over medium-low heat, stirring, until the onion is soft—about five minutes. Transfer the onion to a bowl, and add the bread crumbs, allspice, Worcestershire sauce, egg, ½ teaspoon of salt, and some pepper. Add another 2 tablespoons of the grape juice and stir to form a soft paste.

Spread the paste over the pork, pushing some into the slits. Quarter about eight of the remaining grapes and press them into the stuffing. Reshape the meat and tie it securely into a rolled shape with string.

Put the meat into a roasting bag and place it in a roasting pan. Pour the remaining grape juice into the bag around the meat and tie the bag closed loosely. Make six ½-inch slits in the top of the bag, then cook the pork for one and a half hours.

Cut open the top of the bag, transfer the pork to a cutting board, and cover the meat with foil to keep it warm. Strain the juices from the roasting bag into a saucepan. Dissolve the arrowroot in the Madeira and add it to the pan. Bring the sauce to a boil, stirring constantly, and simmer until it has thickened. Add the remaining grapes and salt, and some pepper, and cook until the grapes are heated through—two to three minutes. Carve the pork into thin slices and serve it with the sauce.

SUGGESTED ACCOMPANIMENT: *red- and green-leaf salad.*

Eastern Scented Tenderloin

Serves 4
Working time: about 30 minutes
Total time: about 1 hour and 20 minutes

Calories **260**
Protein **23g.**
Cholesterol **60mg.**
Total fat **9g.**
Saturated fat **3g.**
Sodium **185mg.**

1 pork tenderloin (about ¾ lb.), trimmed of fat
¼ tsp. salt
½ cinnamon stick
2 tbsp. orange-flower water
½ cup couscous
½ cup dried apricots, soaked in hot water for 20 minutes
¼ cup raisins
2 tbsp. pine nuts, lightly toasted
2 tbsp. chopped fresh tarragon, or 2 tsp. dried tarragon
1 tbsp. chopped fresh mint, or 1 tsp. dried mint
½ tsp. ground coriander
¼ tsp. ground cumin
ground white pepper (optional)
1 tsp. safflower oil
2 tsp. honey

Slit the tenderloin lengthwise with a sharp knife to a depth of half its thickness, and flatten it out as much as possible by pounding it with a mallet *(technique, page 11)*. Season the cut surface with half of the salt.

Bring 1 cup of water to a boil with the cinnamon and flower water. Add the couscous to the liquid; stir for half a minute, cover tightly, and remove it from the heat. After 10 minutes, the couscous will have absorbed all the liquid.

Drain the apricots and chop them coarsely, then combine them in a mixing bowl with the raisins and pine nuts. Remove the cinnamon and mix the couscous with the apricot mixture. Add the tarragon, mint, coriander, and cumin; season with the remaining salt and some white pepper, if you are using it. Carefully stuff the tenderloin with this mixture, reserving any excess filling for serving separately with the cooked meat. Close up the tenderloin and tie carefully around its circumference in six to eight places with string.

Preheat the oven to 375° F. Heat the oil in a large, heavy-bottomed and preferably nonstick frying pan until fairly hot, and brown the meat all over, starting seam side down to seal the opening. Once the pork is brown—five to 10 minutes—brush it all over with the honey and wrap it fairly tightly in foil. Roast the wrapped tenderloin for 20 minutes, then remove it from the oven and allow it to rest for five minutes. Open the foil packet and pour the cooking juices into a small saucepan. Boil the juices until they are reduced to a glaze and then coat the tenderloin with the glaze.

Remove the glazed tenderloin to a hot platter, slice, and serve.

SUGGESTED ACCOMPANIMENTS: *couscous; tomato salad.*

Crépinettes in Mushroom Sauce

THE NAME CRÉPINETTE DERIVES FROM THE FRENCH WORD FOR
CAUL, THE STOMACH MEMBRANE USED TO WRAP
THE MEAT MIXTURE. WHEN BROILED OR FRIED, THE CAUL MELTS
AND KEEPS THE MEAT MOIST DURING COOKING.

Serves 4
Working time: about 40 minutes
Total time: about 1 hour

Calories **280**
Protein **36g.**
Cholesterol **75mg.**
Total fat **13g.**
Saturated fat **4g.**
Sodium **415mg.**

1 lb. pork loin or tenderloin, trimmed of fat
½ cup fresh chestnuts, or 1 oz. dried chestnuts, soaked in water overnight
2 pieces caul (about ⅔ oz.)
4 oz. brown cap mushrooms, or ½ oz. dried porcini (cepes), soaked in hot water for 20 minutes
1 tbsp. cognac (optional)
4 juniper berries, toasted and crushed
1 tsp. coriander seeds, toasted and crushed
½ tsp. yellow mustard seeds, toasted and crushed
1 tsp. salt
freshly ground black pepper

Mushroom sauce

1¼ cup unsalted veal stock (recipe, page 139)
2 tbsp. red wine
2 juniper berries, toasted and crushed
4 oz. brown cap mushrooms, coarsely sliced
2 tbsp. crème fraiche or sour cream
2 tbsp. plain low-fat yogurt

If you are using fresh chestnuts, score the tops and
cook them in boiling water for 20 to 25 minutes, then

drain them and peel off the skins. Soak the caul in acidulated water for a few minutes to soften it. (If the caul has been salted, soak in two or three changes of acidulated water.) Spread the caul out flat and cut it into eight 5-inch squares—exact shaping is unimportant, as are occasional holes.

Preheat the oven to 400° F. Grind or finely chop the pork with the mushrooms. Cut each chestnut into three or four pieces, and mix these into the meat with the cognac, if you are using it, the juniper berries, coriander and mustard seeds, salt, and some pepper. Mix well to distribute the spices evenly.

Form the meat mixture into eight equal egg-shaped patties. Wrap each patty in a square of caul, overlapping the edges to completely enclose each crépinette.

Place the crépinettes in a shallow, ovenproof dish, and for the sauce, add the stock, wine, and juniper berries. Bake for about 25 minutes. Five minutes before the end of the cooking time, drain off the cooking juices into a saucepan and boil rapidly until the liquid is reduced by half. Lower the heat, add the mushrooms and the *crème fraiche* or sour cream, and cook for two to three minutes more. Stir in the yogurt, pour the sauce around the crépinettes, and serve at once.

SUGGESTED ACCOMPANIMENT: *steamed asparagus.*

EDITOR'S NOTE: *For a simpler dish, the mushroom sauce may be omitted and the crépinettes can be broiled for about 10 minutes per side.*

Sesame Schnitzels

TRADITIONALLY, WIENER SCHNITZELS ARE FIRST DIPPED IN BEATEN EGG, THEN COATED WITH WHITE BREAD CRUMBS AND FRIED. THESE LOW-FAT SCHNITZELS HAVE A CRISP, NUTRITIOUS COATING MADE FROM EGG WHITE, BREAD CRUMBS, AND SESAME SEEDS, AND THEY ARE BAKED IN THE OVEN RATHER THAN FRIED.

Serves 4
Working time: about 20 minutes
Total time: about 30 minutes

Calories **420**
Protein **31g.**
Cholesterol **60mg.**
Total fat **21g.**
Saturated fat **3g.**
Sodium **470mg.**

¾ lb. pork tenderloin cutlets (technique, page 12)
⅛ tsp. salt
freshly ground black pepper
2 egg whites
1 cup fine bread crumbs
½ cup sesame seeds
½ tsp. virgin olive oil
8 lemon slices for garnish
12 fresh cranberries, cooked in 1 tbsp. water with 1 tbsp. sugar for 3 to 4 minutes, for garnish (optional)

Place a baking sheet in the oven and preheat the oven to 425° F.

Sprinkle both sides of the cutlets with the salt and a few grindings of black pepper.

Put the egg whites into a shallow dish and whisk with a fork until they are light and frothy. Mix the bread crumbs and sesame seeds together, and spread them out on a flat plate. Dip the cutlets into the beaten egg white, one at a time, and shake off any excess egg white. Then coat the cutlets with the bread-crumb mixture, pressing it firmly onto both sides of the meat with your fingers.

Brush the heated baking sheet with the olive oil and place the meat on it. Cook the schnitzels in the oven, turning them once and pressing frequently with a spatula to keep them flat, until the surfaces are golden and crisp—about 10 minutes.

Arrange the schnitzels on a warmed serving platter, and garnish with the lemon slices and cranberries, if you are using them.

SUGGESTED ACCOMPANIMENT: *colorful mixed-leaf salad with a lemon-flavored dressing.*

Cretan Roast Pork

Serves 6
Working time: about 15 minutes
Total time: about 1 hour and 15 minutes

Calories **190**	
Protein **21g.**	
Cholesterol **70mg.**	
Total fat **9g.**	
Saturated fat **3g.**	
Sodium **333mg.**	

1½ lb. boned pork loin, trimmed of fat, rolled, and tied
1 tbsp. finely chopped fresh oregano, or ½ tsp. dried oregano
1 tsp. salt
freshly ground black pepper
1 tbsp. virgin olive oil
2 garlic cloves, finely chopped
½ lb. plum tomatoes, peeled, seeded, and coarsely chopped
½ cup red wine
2 tbsp. fresh lemon juice

Preheat the oven to 400° F. Rub the surface of the meat with the oregano, salt, and some freshly ground pepper. Heat the oil in a wide, shallow, flameproof casserole over high heat and sear the meat briefly on all sides. Cook the garlic in the oil for a few seconds, then surround the meat with the tomatoes, wine, and lemon juice.

Bake, uncovered, for one hour, turning and basting the meat from time to time with the juices. Also, check occasionally to make sure the tomato mixture does not burn, adding water if necessary.

Transfer the meat to a large serving dish and coat it with the tomato paste before carving it into slices. If any paste remains, serve it as an accompaniment.

SUGGESTED ACCOMPANIMENT: *steamed green beans.*

Lemon Pork

Serves 4
Working time: about 30 minutes
Total time: about 5 hours and 30 minutes
(includes marinating)

Calories **250**
Protein **33g.**
Cholesterol **70mg.**
Total fat **11g.**
Saturated fat **4g.**
Sodium **85mg.**

1 lb. boned pork loin, trimmed of fat
1 lemon
ground white pepper
½ cup basil leaves
1 garlic clove, crushed
3 tbsp. dry white wine

Using a vegetable peeler, remove the zest from the lemon in long strips, working from top to bottom. Put the strips into a pan of cold water, bring to a boil, drain, and refresh the zest under cold running water. Drain well. Cut the strips into threads that can be inserted into a larding needle. Weave some of the threads into the outer surface of the pork, then press the remainder of the threads onto the inner surface. Season the pork inside and out with some white pepper. Roll up the pork and secure with string.

Squeeze the juice from the lemon. Tear the basil leaves into small pieces and place them in a nonreactive dish with the garlic. Place the pork on top, pour the lemon juice over it, cover, and set it aside to marinate in a cool place for four hours, turning the pork occasionally.

Heat the oven to 350° F. Lift the pork from the marinade and place it on a piece of foil. Fold the sides of the foil up, then pour in the marinade and the wine. Fold the foil loosely over the pork and seal the edges together firmly. Place the parcel on a baking sheet and cook it in the oven until the pork is tender—approximately 40 minutes.

Transfer the pork to a warmed plate, cover, and let it rest. In a saucepan, boil the cooking juices until they are slightly thickened.

Slice the pork, divide the slices among four warmed plates, and spoon the juices around the meat.

SUGGESTED ACCOMPANIMENT: *steamed sliced zucchini.*

Oriental Pot Roast

Serves 12
Working time: about 30 minutes
Total time: about 2 hours and 45 minutes

Calories **220**
Protein **32g.**
Cholesterol **70mg.**
Total fat **8g.**
Saturated fat **3g.**
Sodium **310mg.**

3 lb. boned pork loin, trimmed of fat and tied into shape
1 tbsp. safflower oil
2 tbsp. very finely chopped fresh ginger
2 tbsp. very finely chopped garlic
1 tbsp. very finely chopped fresh green chili pepper (caution, page 36)
4 tbsp. rice wine or dry sherry
2 tsp. brown sugar
4 tbsp. low-sodium soy sauce
2 sweet red peppers, seeded and deribbed, each cut into 12 strips
24 frozen baby corn
24 small scallions

Brown the meat well on all sides in a very hot, dry wok or a heavy-bottomed skillet. It may seem to stick at first, but if you leave the stuck surface for a few seconds and the heat is high enough, the meat will soon loosen. Keep the wok unwashed for later use.

Heat the oil in a flameproof casserole, then add the ginger, garlic, and chili pepper. Stir until the mixture begins to brown, then add the rice wine or sherry, and bring to a boil. Reduce the heat to low. Stir in the sugar and soy sauce, then place the browned meat in the casserole and turn it in the mixture so that all sides are coated. Ensure that the heat is low enough so that the liquid does not boil, cover the pot, and cook for two and a quarter hours. Add a little stock or water, if necessary, to prevent the meat from sticking.

About 15 minutes before serving, stir-fry first the red-pepper strips, then the corn, and finally the scallions in the wok or skillet over high heat. Transfer each batch to a bowl after stir-frying. The vegetables should be slightly soft and flecked with black, but still crisp.

When the meat has finished cooking, remove the string and slice the meat into 12 portions. Lay the slices on a serving platter. If the liquid in the casserole has not reduced to a dark, glossy syrup, skim off any fat and reduce the liquid over high heat. Toss the vegetables in the syrup left at the bottom of the casserole and make sure they are heated through, then spoon them over the pork and serve immediately.

SUGGESTED ACCOMPANIMENTS: *rice; bok choy in oyster sauce.*

Green Peppercorn Tenderloin

Serves 4
Working time: about 35 minutes
Total time: about 1 hour and 20 minutes

Calories **180**
Protein **19g.**
Cholesterol **60mg.**
Total fat **9g.**
Saturated fat **3g.**
Sodium **240mg.**

¾ lb. pork tenderloin, trimmed of fat
¼ lb. button mushrooms
2 shallots
1 tsp. virgin olive oil
3 tbsp. fresh lemon juice
½ tsp. salt
½ cup green beans, trimmed
1 tsp. green peppercorns packed in brine, rinsed and drained
1 tbsp. chopped fresh marjoram, or 1 tsp. dried marjoram
1 cup unsalted chicken stock (recipe, page 139)
1 cup dry white wine
1 tsp. cornstarch

Preheat the oven to 375° F. Cut a lengthwise slit about halfway into the pork tenderloin, then open the pork out and place it, cut side down, on a board. Cover with a piece of plastic wrap and pound with a wooden mallet until the pork has a rectangular shape and is about ½ inch thick (*technique, page 11*).

Chop the mushrooms and shallots finely in a food processor or by hand. Heat the oil in a nonstick frying pan, and add the mushrooms and shallots and 1 tablespoon of the lemon juice. Cook over medium heat, stirring frequently, until almost all of the moisture has evaporated—about seven minutes. Remove the pan from the heat and stir in the salt. Set aside.

Blanch the beans in boiling water for three minutes. Drain the beans and refresh them under cold water, then drain them again and dry them on paper towels.

Spread the mushroom mixture over the pork, leaving about ¼ inch clear on all sides. Sprinkle the peppercorns evenly over the mushroom mixture, then arrange the beans on top, parallel to the long edges of the meat. Press the beans into the mushroom mixture and sprinkle the marjoram over the beans.

Roll up the pork from a long side and tie it into shape with string. Place the pork in a roasting pan and pour the stock over it, along with half of the wine and the remaining lemon juice. Roast the pork for 45 minutes, basting several times with the cooking juices.

Remove the pork from the pan and keep it warm. Bring the cooking liquid to a simmer over medium heat. Mix the cornstarch with the remaining wine and stir this into the simmering liquid. Cook, stirring, for two minutes. Strain the sauce into a gravy boat.

Put the pork on a cutting board, cut away the string, and slice the pork into rounds. Arrange the slices on a heated serving plate and serve with the sauce.

Tenderloin Persillé with Carrot Puree

Serves 4
Working time: about 40 minutes
Total time: about 50 minutes

Calories **230**
Protein **22g.**
Cholesterol **75mg.**
Total fat **9g.**
Saturated fat **4g.**
Sodium **380mg.**

1 lb. pork tenderloin, trimmed of fat
½ tsp. salt
freshly ground black pepper
2 tbsp. Dijon mustard
4 tbsp. finely chopped parsley
¼ cup fine dry white bread crumbs
¾ lb. carrots
¼ cup fresh orange juice
1½ tsp. unsalted butter, chilled and cut into tiny cubes

Preheat the oven to 400° F. Wipe the tenderloin dry, and season it with the salt and some pepper. Brown the meat all over in a hot, dry nonstick frying pan. Brush the whole tenderloin with the mustard and sprinkle the parsley on all sides; roll the tenderloin in the bread crumbs so that it is evenly coated. Place the pork on a wire rack in a roasting pan and cook it in the oven for 30 to 40 minutes, until the crumbs are brown and the juices run clear when the meat is pierced.

Steam the carrots until they are tender, then puree them with the orange juice in a food processor or by passing them through a sieve. Heat the puree slowly in a small saucepan, then gradually beat in the butter.

Let the tenderloin rest for 10 minutes, then carve it into thick slices and serve it with the carrot puree.

SUGGESTED ACCOMPANIMENTS: *new potatoes; green beans.*

EDITOR'S NOTE: *The tenderloin may also be served cold, cut into thin slices and accompanied by a vinaigrette.*

Herbed Roast Tenderloin of Pork with Three Purees

Serves 4
Working (and total) time: about 40 minutes

Calories **285**
Protein **25g.**
Cholesterol **80mg.**
Total fat **12g.**
Saturated fat **5g.**
Sodium **420mg.**

1 lb. pork tenderloin, trimmed of fat
1 tbsp. unsalted butter, softened
½ tsp. salt
freshly ground black pepper
1 tsp. chopped fresh tarragon, or ½ tsp. dried tarragon
1½ tsp. chopped flat-leaf parsley
1 tbsp. safflower oil
½ lemon, juice only
2½ cups unsalted chicken stock (recipe, page 139) or water
¾ lb. carrots, peeled and coarsely chopped
⅓ lb. potatoes, peeled and coarsely chopped
⅓ lb. celeriac, peeled and coarsely chopped
⅓ lb. beets, peeled and coarsely chopped
⅓ lb. new white turnips, peeled and coarsely chopped
½ cup milk
2 sprigs chervil or parsley, torn into pieces

Preheat the oven to 450° F. With a knife, cut a deep lengthwise slit in the pork to within about ½ inch of the opposite side. Spread the butter inside the pocket, add the salt and some pepper, and stuff the pocket with the tarragon and parsley. Close up the pocket by tying string around the tenderloin at intervals of about 1½ inches. Heat the oil in a heavy-bottomed pan over medium heat and brown the tenderloin all over. Remove the meat from the pan, put it on a piece of foil, pour the lemon juice over it, then wrap it loosely.

Place the tenderloin in the oven to cook for 25 minutes. Divide the stock or water among three saucepans and bring to a boil; cook the carrots in the first pan, the potatoes and celeriac in the second, and the beets and turnips in the third until they are soft.

When the vegetables are soft, drain them, reserving the cooking liquid. In a food processor, puree the carrots with a little of their reserved cooking liquid, then puree the potatoes and celeriac with the milk, and the beets and turnips with a little reserved cooking liquid. Return each puree to its cooking pan. When the pork is cooked, warm the purees over low heat. Cut the tenderloin into thin slices, and either arrange these on a large serving plate and pass the purees separately, or divide the pork among four plates with the purees spooned around it. Garnish with the chervil or parsley.

EDITOR'S NOTE: *The purees can be prepared in advance and refrigerated until they are needed.*

2
Under the lid of an Oriental steaming basket, meatballs of pork and bulgur (recipe, page 97) are evenly arranged on the bamboo latticework.

Balancing the Flavors

Cooking meat in a liquid precipitates a gradual exchange of benefits—as the meat's juices are released, the meat in turn absorbs the flavors in the liquid around it. In the recipes in this chapter, the disparate ingredients—meat, vegetables, fruit, herbs, spices, liquids—all contribute to this transaction, inviting the cook to create from their unique characteristics a harmonious whole. The method may be as simple as cooking all the ingredients together for a specified time, as is the case with the Indian stew on page 80. More often, the process involves several stages to allow for the different cooking times of the various constituents, but the aim is always the same: a balanced interplay of flavors and textures in which no one element overwhelms or detracts from another.

Poaching and braising are both methods customarily employed to cook tougher cuts of meat that require lengthy cooking to break down their connective tissue, but they are equally appropriate for the tenderloin and loin cuts that feature in many of the recipes that follow. In poaching, the meat is completely immersed in a liquid and cooked over low heat on top of the stove. Because boiling causes meat to become tough and stringy, it is important to maintain the liquid at a constant simmer—the surface should be just trembling, with bubbles drifting slowly up. Any fat that melts out of the meat during cooking should be carefully skimmed off.

Braises require less liquid and may be cooked either on the stove or in the oven. When the meat is cut into pieces, it is usually described as a stew. Before the liquid is added, the meat is often seared at a high temperature—large cuts in the oven, small cuts and pieces on the stove—to give its surface an appetizing brown crust. The meat may also be tenderized in a marinade that is later added to the cooking liquid, and larger cuts may be stuffed. The cooking liquid itself is often stock, wine, or water, but beer *(page 75)*, cider *(page 78)*, and even milk *(page 67)* are all appropriate liquids for pork.

A number of recipes in this chapter call for a steamer, a pan with one or two perforated containers in which the food is cooked by steam rising from the boiling liquid beneath it. Steaming is particularly suitable for delicate foods such as the pork and bulgur meatballs shown at left and on page 97. In another recipe, stuffed pork steaks are steamed over boiling stock and fennel *(page 95)*; and in the couscous dish on page 96, the pork is cooked with vegetables over boiling water and ginger while the couscous steams in the second container above them—a progressive transfusion of flavors that elevates the final assembly into far more than the sum of its parts.

White-Cabbage Pork

Serves 4
Working time: about 30 minutes
Total time: about 8 hours (includes marinating)

Calories **250**
Protein **23g.**
Cholesterol **70mg.**
Total fat **11g.**
Saturated fat **3g.**
Sodium **185mg.**

1 lb. boned pork loin, trimmed of fat
1½ tsp. caraway seeds
1¼ cups apple juice
1 tbsp. safflower oil
1 small onion, finely chopped
1 lb. white cabbage, shredded
¼ tsp. salt
ground white pepper
1 small red-skinned apple for garnish
dill sprigs for garnish

Unroll the loin and sprinkle half of the caraway seeds evenly over the inside. Then roll it up and tie it with string. Place the pork in a nonreactive bowl and sprinkle the remaining caraway seeds over it, then pour in the apple juice. Cover and let the pork marinate in a cool place for six hours, turning it occasionally.

Preheat the oven to 325° F. Remove the pork from the bowl and pat it dry; reserve the apple juice. Heat a flameproof casserole on high, add the oil, and brown the pork. Transfer the meat to a plate. Reduce the heat to low, add the onion to the casserole, and cook, stirring frequently, for three to four minutes. Add the cabbage in batches and cook each batch, stirring frequently, for two to three minutes; transfer each batch to a bowl before cooking the next. When all the cabbage is cooked, stir to distribute the onion. Set the pork on a layer of cabbage and onion in the casserole, and surround it with the remaining cabbage and onion. Bring the reserved juice to a boil, add the salt and some white pepper, then pour it over the pork.

Cover the casserole tightly and cook in the oven until the pork is tender—about 45 minutes. Transfer the pork to a warmed plate, cover, and let it rest for about 10 minutes. Meanwhile, core and slice the apple.

Slice the pork. Arrange the cabbage on a warmed dish, place the pork on top, and spoon the cooking juices over it. Garnish with the dill and apple slices.

Pork Cooked in Milk

Serves 4
Working time: about 20 minutes
Total time: about 1 hour and 10 minutes

Calories **265**
Protein **35g.**
Cholesterol **70mg.**
Total fat **11g.**
Saturated fat **5g.**
Sodium **135mg.**

1 lb. boned pork loin, trimmed of fat, rolled, and tied
1 onion, finely chopped
3 tbsp. unsalted veal or chicken stock (recipes, page 139), or 3 tbsp. water
2 bay leaves, broken
1 small sprig thyme, or ¼ tsp. dried thyme leaves
1 sprig parsley
¼ tsp. salt
freshly ground black pepper
1½ cups skim milk

In a heavy-bottomed, nonstick pan or a flameproof casserole, simmer the onion in the stock or water until the onion is soft and the liquid is evaporated—three to four minutes. Add the bay leaves, thyme, and parsley, and place the pork on top; season with the salt and some pepper, then gradually pour in the milk. Bring the liquid to a boil, then lower the heat and simmer, covered, for about 45 minutes, until the pork is just tender and the milk well reduced—a skin should form on the milk's surface. Lift the pork out with a slotted spoon and keep it warm. Continue to simmer the sauce, if necessary, until about 6 tablespoons remain.

Carve the pork into slices and divide it among four warmed plates. Remove the herb sprigs from the sauce and spoon one-quarter of the sauce onto each plate.

SUGGESTED ACCOMPANIMENT: *new potatoes with parsley.*

Rolled Cutlets with Eggplant

Serves 4
Working time: about 1 hour
Total time: about 3 hours (includes marinating)

Calories **168**
Protein **20g.**
Cholesterol **65mg.**
Total fat **20g.**
Saturated fat **3g.**
Sodium **205mg.**

4 pork cutlets (about 3 oz. each)
½ tsp. finely chopped fresh sage
1 tsp. fresh thyme leaves
freshly ground black pepper
1 lb. eggplant
½ tsp. salt
1½ tbsp. virgin olive oil
2 garlic cloves, finely chopped
1 lb. ripe plum tomatoes, peeled, seeded, and chopped, or 10 oz. canned whole tomatoes, drained and chopped

Pound the cutlets to tenderize them *(page 12, Step 2)*. Sprinkle the meat evenly on both sides with the sage, thyme, and some pepper, and let it absorb the flavors for 30 minutes to one hour.

Meanwhile, cut the stem off the eggplant and peel off half the skin in alternate lengthwise strips. Cut the eggplant diagonally into ¼-inch-thick slices; sprinkle the slices evenly with ¼ teaspoon of the salt and let them drain in a colander for at least 30 minutes.

Preheat the oven to 425° F. Rinse the eggplant slices well under cold running water, then press each slice firmly between your hands so that the spongy texture is broken down and it becomes waxy in appearance. Dry the slices thoroughly on paper towels.

Cover each cutlet with a slice of eggplant, then roll each cutlet up tightly, beginning at one of its shorter edges, into a neat, chubby sausage shape; secure with wooden picks.

Arrange the rolled cutlets in a single layer in an ovenproof gratin dish, brush them with half of the oil, and bake, uncovered, for 30 minutes, turning once so that all sides are evenly colored.

In the meantime, heat the remaining olive oil in a heavy-bottomed frying pan over medium-high heat. Cut the remaining eggplant slices into small dice and sauté these with the garlic until the eggplant is well colored. Add the ripe or canned tomatoes and ⅛ teaspoon of the remaining salt, and continue cooking until the mixture is well reduced and thick—approximately 10 minutes.

When the rolled pork cutlets are golden brown, lower the oven temperature to 375° F. Pour the tomato mixture over the meat, cover the dish with foil, and braise for one hour.

Transfer the meat rolls to a warm serving plate, take out the wooden picks, and trim the ends of the rolls to expose the spirals of eggplant. Sprinkle the rolls with the remaining salt. Transfer the contents of the gratin dish to a saucepan and reduce the mixture over medium heat until it is thick. Spoon the sauce over the meat before serving.

SUGGESTED ACCOMPANIMENTS: *steamed saffron rice; salad of crisp leaves.*

Red-Cabbage Pork

Serves 4
Working time: about 30 minutes
Total time: about 2 hours

Calories **310**
Protein **37g.**
Cholesterol **110mg.**
Total fat **13g.**
Saturated fat **4g.**
Sodium **170mg.**

1½ lb. boned pork loin
1 tbsp. safflower oil
1 onion, finely chopped
1 lb. red cabbage, shredded
2 firm pears, peeled and thickly sliced
3 cloves
1 tsp. sugar
3 tbsp. fresh lemon juice
2 strips lemon zest, each about 2 inches long

Preheat the oven to 325° F. Trim the pork loin of all visible fat and roll it, tying it with string in several places. Heat the safflower oil in a heavy, flameproof casserole over high heat, add the pork, and cook for about three minutes, turning the pork so that it browns evenly. Transfer the meat to a plate.

Lower the heat, add the onion to the casserole, and cook, stirring frequently and scraping up the caramelized juices from the bottom of the casserole, until the onion is soft—three to four minutes. Add the cabbage in batches and cook, stirring frequently, for about two minutes per batch. Transfer each batch to a plate before cooking the next batch.

Mix the red cabbage and onion, pears, cloves, and sugar together in a bowl, then make a thick bed of about half of the cabbage mixture in the bottom of the casserole. Add the lemon juice and the strips of lemon zest. Place the pork on top, and pack the remaining cabbage mixture around the meat and over the top. Cover the casserole and cook it in the oven for one hour and 20 minutes.

Transfer the pork loin to a warmed plate, cover it, and set it aside to rest. Spoon off the juices from the red cabbage and boil them for several minutes to reduce them slightly.

Carve the pork into slices and divide the slices among four warmed plates. Add the cabbage, and spoon the juices over the pork and cabbage.

Mango Pork

Serves 8
Working time: about 35 minutes
Total time: about 2 hours and 15 minutes

Calories **270**
Protein **33g.**
Cholesterol **70mg.**
Total fat **13g.**
Saturated fat **4g.**
Sodium **115mg.**

2 lb. boned pork loin, trimmed of fat, rolled, and tied
1 tbsp. virgin olive oil
½ onion, finely chopped
1 carrot, chopped
1 celery rib, chopped
1 garlic clove, chopped
1 tbsp. chopped fresh ginger
1 tbsp. coriander seeds
12 cardamom pods, lightly crushed to open
1 tsp. cumin seeds
½ tsp. black peppercorns
½ cinnamon stick
1 dried chili pepper, halved (caution, page 36)
1¼ cups unsalted chicken stock (recipe, page 139)
½ cup dry sherry
1 ripe mango, peeled and chopped
½ lemon, juice only (optional)
½ cucumber, halved lengthwise and thinly sliced, for garnish
½ cup cilantro sprigs, stalks removed, leaves torn into small pieces, for garnish

Preheat the oven to 350° F. Heat the oil in a medium-size, deep, flameproof casserole over medium-low heat; add the onion, carrot, celery, garlic, and ginger. Cover and cook on low, stirring occasionally, until the vegetables are soft—five to seven minutes.

Add the coriander, cardamom pods, cumin seeds,

peppercorns, cinnamon, and chili pepper, and stir to mix with the vegetables. Place the pork loin on top. Pour in the stock and sherry, and bring to a boil; then cover tightly and transfer to the oven. Braise for one and a half hours.

Remove the pork from the casserole and scrape off any spices or vegetables that have stuck to it. Wrap the pork in foil and set it aside while you make the sauce.

Strain the cooking liquid into a saucepan, pressing down on the vegetables and spices in the sieve to extract all their flavorings; discard the contents of the sieve. Put the mango into a food processor with about half of the strained cooking liquid, and puree the mixture. Press the puree through the sieve into the saucepan containing the remaining cooking liquid, and stir to mix. Add the lemon juice, if you are using it, then reheat the sauce over low heat.

Slice the pork into thin rounds and arrange on hot plates with the sauce poured around or spooned over the pork. Garnish with the cucumber slices and the cilantro leaves.

Sorrel Paupiettes

Serves 4
Working (and total) time: about 50 minutes

Calories **235**
Protein **35g.**
Cholesterol **85mg.**
Total fat **14g.**
Saturated fat **4g.**
Sodium **280mg.**

¾ lb. pork cutlets (2 large or 4 small), trimmed of fat
¼ lb. lean pork for chopping
2 cups fresh sorrel leaves, deveined
1 small bunch each of fresh sage, thyme, and marjoram
½ tsp. green peppercorns in brine, rinsed and drained
½ tsp. salt
freshly ground black pepper
2 tbsp. pistachio nuts
1 tsp. safflower oil
1½ tsp. unsalted butter
1 cup unsalted chicken stock (recipe, page 139)
Mustard and sorrel sauce
¼ tsp. arrowroot
1 tbsp. unsalted chicken stock (recipe, page 139) or water
⅓ cup plain low-fat yogurt
2 tsp. grainy mustard
¼ tsp. salt
1 cup shredded fresh sorrel leaves

Pound the pork cutlets until they are double their original size (page 12, Step 2); if you are using large cutlets, cut them in half.

Plunge the sorrel leaves into boiling water and refresh them immediately in cold running water. Dry the leaves carefully on a clean tea towel or paper towels. Cover one side of each cutlet with sorrel leaves.

In a food processor, finely chop the lean pork with the sage, thyme, marjoram, peppercorns, salt, and some pepper. Transfer the chopped pork mixture to a

nonstick pan and cook for about five minutes, stirring continuously. Allow it to cool slightly, then spread one-quarter of the mixture onto the leaf-coated side of each cutlet. Arrange one-quarter of the pistachio nuts toward one end of each cutlet and roll up the meat into paupiettes, starting at the pistachio end. The bundles should hold together without tying, but if not, secure gently with string.

Heat the safflower oil and butter together in a heavy-bottomed frying pan with a lid over medium heat. Place the paupiettes carefully in the pan, seam side down, and cook them until they are browned—about six minutes, covering if the meat is in danger of burning, and turning the paupiettes from time to time once the seams have sealed. Meanwhile, warm the stock over low heat.

Remove the paupiettes and wipe the pan surface with paper towels to remove residual fat. Replace the meat in the pan and add the stock. Simmer over very low heat (a rapid boil will toughen the meat) until the meat is tender—about five minutes.

Remove the paupiettes from the pan, discard any string, and keep the paupiettes warm while you make the sauce. Dissolve the arrowroot in the stock or water, and stir the mixture into the cooking liquid in the pan. Cook over low heat for a minute or two until it is slightly thickened and clear. Remove the pan from the heat, and beat in the yogurt and mustard. Season with the salt, then add the meat and warm through over very low heat. Immediately before serving, stir in the shredded sorrel. Serve hot, slicing each paupiette before serving, if you wish.

SUGGESTED ACCOMPANIMENTS: *new or baked potatoes; steamed spinach.*

EDITOR'S NOTE: *If sorrel is not available, young spinach leaves may be used instead.*

Loin Chops with Mushrooms and Sherry

Serves 4
Working time: about 35 minutes
Total time: about 1 hour and 20 minutes

Calories **270**
Protein **36g.**
Cholesterol **70mg.**
Total fat **12g.**
Saturated fat **5g.**
Sodium **300mg.**

4 loin chops (4½ to 5 oz. each), trimmed of fat
½ tsp. salt
freshly ground black pepper
1 onion, finely chopped
1 garlic clove, very finely chopped
1 lb. button mushrooms, finely chopped
¼ cup dry sherry
2 large sorrel leaves, deveined, cut into thin strips
⅓ cup plain low-fat yogurt

Season the chops with the salt and some pepper, then brown them well on both sides in a nonstick frying pan over medium heat. Transfer the chops to a heavy, flameproof casserole.

Cook the onion and garlic, covered, in the frying pan until they are soft but not brown—about three min-utes. Add them to the loin chops in the casserole.

Put the mushrooms into the frying pan, turn up the heat, and stir as they begin to cook. When almost all of their juice has evaporated, pour in the sherry and boil until it is reduced by three-quarters—about two minutes. Transfer the mushrooms to the casserole.

Bring the contents of the casserole to a boil, then reduce the heat to low, cover, and let the chops sim-mer until they are tender—approximately 45 minutes. When they are done, remove the chops and keep them warm, scraping off and returning any pieces of veg-etable to the casserole.

Increase the heat under the mushroom mixture and boil until almost all of the liquid is evaporated. Stir in the sorrel leaves, then remove the casserole from the heat and stir in the yogurt. Serve the chops immedi-ately on individual plates, with a large spoonful of the mushroom mixture on top of each chop.

SUGGESTED ACCOMPANIMENT: *steamed broccoli.*

EDITOR'S NOTE: *If you do not have sorrel, substitute spinach leaves and stir in 1 teaspoon of lemon juice with the yogurt.*

Pork Cooked like Game

Serves 4
Working time: about 30 minutes
Total time: about 1 day (includes marinating)

Calories **220**
Protein **22g.**
Cholesterol **70mg.**
Total fat **7g.**
Saturated fat **3g.**
Sodium **115mg.**

1 lb. boned pork loin, trimmed of fat and rolled
1 oz. dried porcini (cepes)
1 onion, sliced
Juniper marinade
1 small onion, finely chopped
1 small carrot, diced
10 juniper berries
4 black peppercorns, lightly crushed
1 bay leaf, broken in half
1 small sprig rosemary
1 sprig thyme
1 sprig parsley
1¼ cups red wine

To make the marinade, scatter the onion and carrot in the bottom of a nonreactive dish. Lay the pork on top, add the juniper berries, peppercorns, bay leaf, rosemary, thyme, and parsley, then pour the wine over the meat. Cover the dish and let the pork marinate in the refrigerator for 24 hours, turning it occasionally.

Pour 1 cup of boiling water over the porcini and let them soak for 20 minutes. Remove the mushrooms from the liquid and reserve the liquid.

Preheat the oven to 325° F. Lift the pork from the marinade; reserve the marinade. On top of the stove, heat a heavy, nonstick flameproof casserole; add the pork and cook over high heat, turning the pork so that it browns evenly all over. Transfer the pork to a plate. Add the sliced onion to the casserole and cook over low heat, stirring frequently and scraping the caramelized meat juices from the bottom of the casserole, until it is slightly soft—two to three minutes. Return the pork to the casserole, add the mushrooms, then pour the mushroom-soaking liquid and the marinade over the pork so that it is almost covered. Increase the heat and bring the liquid to a simmer.

Cover the casserole tightly, transfer it to the oven, and cook for 40 to 45 minutes. When the meat is cooked, transfer it to a warmed plate, cover, and let it rest in a low oven.

Strain the cooking liquid; discard the bay leaf and herb sprigs, but reserve the vegetables. Skim off any fat from the surface of the liquid, then reduce it by about three-quarters.

Slice the pork. Accompany each serving with some of the reserved vegetables and the reduced sauce.

Chops with Spiced Orange Sauce

Serves 4
Working time: about 20 minutes
Total time: about 35 minutes

Calories **200**
Protein **21g.**
Cholesterol **70mg.**
Total fat **8g.**
Saturated fat **3g.**
Sodium **275mg.**

4 boned pork loin chops (about 4 oz. each), trimmed of fat
2 shallots, finely chopped
1 small green pepper, seeded, deribbed, and cut into thin strips
¼ tsp. ground cinnamon
⅛ tsp. ground cloves
3 large oranges, juice and grated zest of two, the third peeled and thinly sliced
1 tbsp. brown sugar
2 tsp. arrowroot
½ tsp. salt
freshly ground black pepper

In a large, nonstick frying pan, cook the chops over high heat until they are browned—about three minutes, turning once. Add the shallots and green pepper, and continue to cook, stirring, for two minutes. Stir in the cinnamon and cloves.

Put the orange juice into a measuring cup and add enough water to make 1 cup. Add the liquid to the pan along with the orange zest and sugar. Bring the liquid to a boil, then lower the heat and simmer for 10 minutes, until the chops are tender.

Using a slotted spoon, transfer the pork chops to a serving plate and keep them warm. Add the orange slices to the pan and heat them through. In a small bowl or cup, mix the arrowroot with 2 tablespoons of cold water; add it to the pan and stir until the sauce thickens. Season with the salt and some pepper. Spoon the sauce around the pork before serving.

Pork Carbonnade

Serves 8
Working time: about 40 minutes
Total time: about 2 hours and 20 minutes

Calories **480**
Protein **38g.**
Cholesterol **70mg.**
Total fat **25g.**
Saturated fat **6g.**
Sodium **550mg.**

2 lb. lean pork shoulder, trimmed of fat and cut into bite-size pieces
4 tbsp. flour
2 tbsp. polyunsaturated margarine
3 tbsp. safflower oil
3 large onions, halved and sliced
3 garlic cloves, crushed
1¾ cups unsalted chicken stock (recipe, page 139)
1¾ cups beer
3 tsp. wine vinegar
1 tsp. salt
freshly ground black pepper
1 bouquet garni
8 slices French bread, ½ inch thick
1½ tbsp. mustard
3 tbsp. chopped parsley
3 oz. reduced-fat Cheddar-flavor cheese, grated
fresh bay leaves for garnish (optional)

Preheat the oven to 350° F.

Toss the pork in the flour until the pieces are thoroughly coated. Heat half of the margarine with the safflower oil in a large saucepan over medium-low heat, and cook the onions with two of the crushed garlic cloves for three minutes.

Using a slotted spoon, transfer the onions and garlic to a casserole. Increase the heat to medium high and add the pork to the pan, reserving any excess flour. Fry the pork, turning the cubes until they are seared all over; stir in any remaining flour and cook for one minute. Gradually add the stock and beer and bring the mixture to a simmer, stirring all the time. Add the vinegar, salt, and some pepper, pour the mixture over the onions in the casserole, then add the bouquet garni. Cover the casserole and cook in the oven for one and a half hours.

Meanwhile, prepare the topping. Toast the slices of French bread on one side only. Mix the remaining margarine with the mustard, 2 tablespoons of the chopped parsley, and the remaining garlic. Spread the mixture over the untoasted sides of the bread.

At the end of its cooking time, remove the casserole from the oven and discard the bouquet garni. Arrange the slices of bread, toasted sides down, on top of the casserole, pushing each slice into the mixture to moisten it. Sprinkle with the grated Cheddar cheese, then bake, uncovered, until the topping is golden—approximately 25 minutes. Sprinkle with the remaining chopped parsley and garnish with the fresh bay leaves, if you are using them.

Light Gumbo

Serves 4
Working time: about 30 minutes
Total time: about 2 hours

Calories **290**
Protein **40g.**
Cholesterol **145mg.**
Total fat **13g.**
Saturated fat **5g.**
Sodium **370mg.**

¾ lb. lean pork, trimmed of fat and cut into ½-inch cubes
1 lb. cooked shrimp, unpeeled
3 sprigs parsley
½ tsp. black peppercorns
½ tsp. salt
1 onion, finely chopped
1 garlic clove, crushed
1 lb. okra, trimmed and cut into 1-inch slices
1 fresh green chili pepper, finely chopped (caution, page 36)
1 lb. tomatoes, peeled, seeded, and cut into fine strips
3 tbsp. finely chopped cilantro, or 3 tbsp. chopped parsley, plus 2 tbsp. fresh lime juice

Remove the heads and shells from the shrimp and set the flesh aside. Put the shells and heads into a pan with 1 quart of water, the parsley sprigs, and peppercorns; bring to a boil. Lower the heat, cover the pan, and simmer for 20 minutes. Strain the stock through a sieve and set it aside; discard the solids in the sieve.

Brown the meat in a dry, nonstick frying pan over medium-high heat, stir in the salt, then add the onion and garlic, and cook with the pork until the onion softens—about five minutes. Put the contents of the frying pan and the stock into a saucepan and bring to a boil. Cover and let it simmer until the meat is very tender—about one and a half hours.

Toss the okra in a wok or a dry, nonstick skillet over high heat until it is charred in places but still green and crisp. Stir in the chili pepper and cook briefly; transfer the okra and chili to the stew with the tomatoes, the cilantro or parsley, the lime juice, and the shrimp. Bring the stew quickly to a boil; serve immediately.

SUGGESTED ACCOMPANIMENT: *crusty bread or boiled rice.*

EDITOR'S NOTE: *Gumbo is usually served in bowls as a soup or stew and eaten with spoons.*

Pork Stroganoff

NAMED AFTER A 19TH-CENTURY RUSSIAN DIPLOMAT, STROGANOFF IS TRADITIONALLY A BEEF DISH WITH ONIONS AND MUSHROOMS IN A THICK SOUR-CREAM SAUCE. IN THIS LIGHT ADAPTATION FOR PORK, YOGURT REPLACES THE SOUR CREAM.

Serves 4
Working (and total) time: about 25 minutes

Calories **250**
Protein **24g.**
Cholesterol **70mg.**
Total fat **14g.**
Saturated fat **4g.**
Sodium **190mg.**

1 lb. pork tenderloin, trimmed of fat and cut into thin strips
1½ tbsp. safflower oil
1 large onion, quartered and thinly sliced
6 oz. button mushrooms, sliced
2 tbsp. whole wheat flour
1¼ cups unsalted chicken stock (recipe, page 139)
1 tbsp. tomato paste
1 tsp. fresh lemon juice
¼ tsp. salt
freshly ground black pepper
¼ cup plain low-fat yogurt

Heat the oil in a large frying pan over medium-high heat until it is hot but not smoking, add the pork strips and onion, and cook, stirring frequently, until the pork is browned all over—about three minutes. Stir in the mushrooms and cook for one minute more, stirring.

Add the flour to the pan and mix well, then gradually stir in the stock and bring to a boil, stirring all the time. Lower the heat and simmer for two minutes, then stir in the tomato paste, lemon juice, salt, and some pepper. Heat the mixture through over low heat for two minutes. Remove the pan from the heat, stir in the yogurt, and serve immediately.

SUGGESTED ACCOMPANIMENT: *whole wheat or spinach fettuccine.*

Pork Hot Pot

Serves 8
Working time: about 40 minutes
Total time: about 4 hours and 30 minutes
(includes soaking)

Calories **365**	
Protein **25g.**	2 lb. pork tenderloin, trimmed of fat and cut into chunks
Cholesterol **70mg.**	3 cups dry cider
Total fat **9g.**	2 cinnamon sticks
Saturated fat **3g.**	12 allspice berries
Sodium **400mg.**	16 cloves
	24 black peppercorns
	2 oranges, pared zest only
	¼ lb. dried pears
	3 lb. new potatoes, scrubbed and sliced
	½ lb. small carrots, halved crosswise and then quartered lengthwise
	1 lb. small leeks, sliced
	2 ribs celery, chopped
	½ cup golden raisins
	1 tsp. salt

Put the cider into a nonreactive saucepan with the cinnamon, allspice, cloves, peppercorns, and orange zest, and bring to a boil. Remove from the heat, cover, and let the mixture infuse for 30 minutes.

Add the pears to the liquid and set them aside to soak, uncovered, for one hour.

Remove the pears with a slotted spoon and cut them crosswise into strips; set aside. Strain and reserve the liquid, and discard the spices and flavorings.

Preheat the oven to 325° F.

Grease the bottom of a casserole. Arrange about one-third of the potato slices in a layer over the bottom, then layer the carrots, pork, leeks, celery, and golden raisins in the casserole. Scatter the strips of pear over the top. Stir the salt into the cider and pour the cider into the casserole, then arrange the remaining potato slices on top, overlapping them slightly to make a neat topping.

Cover the casserole and cook it in the oven for one hour and 45 minutes, then remove the lid; tilt the casserole and spoon the liquid over the top layer of potatoes. Return the casserole to the oven, uncovered, and cook for another 40 minutes to brown the surface of the potatoes.

Portuguese Pork

PORTUGUESE COOKING IS NOTED FOR ITS USE OF PEAS, WHICH
ARE A GOOD SOURCE OF VITAMINS, PROTEIN, AND FIBER.

Serves 4
Working time: about 30 minutes
Total time: about 1 hour and 15 minutes

Calories **350**
Protein **28g.**
Cholesterol **70mg.**
Total fat **14g.**
Saturated fat **4g.**
Sodium **135mg.**

1 lb. pork tenderloin, trimmed of fat and sliced into thick rounds
1 tbsp. safflower oil
1 large onion, thinly sliced
2 garlic cloves, crushed
1½ lb. plum tomatoes, quartered, or 14 oz. canned whole tomatoes, drained
2 tbsp. tomato paste
⅔ cup dry white wine
⅔ cup unsalted vegetable or chicken stock (recipes, page 139)
2 tbsp. chopped parsley
2 tbsp. chopped fresh basil
1 tsp. dried mixed herbs
½ tsp. sugar
⅛ tsp. salt
freshly ground black pepper
½ lb. fresh or frozen peas
1 sweet yellow pepper, seeded, deribbed, and thinly sliced lengthwise

Heat the oil in a heavy, flameproof casserole over medium heat, add the onion, and cook, stirring, until the onion begins to brown—about five minutes. Stir in the garlic, tomatoes, tomato paste, wine, and stock. Bring the mixture to a boil, stirring, then lower the heat, and add half of the parsley and basil, the dried mixed herbs, sugar, salt, and some pepper. Simmer uncovered, stirring occasionally, until the sauce is reduced and quite thick—about 20 minutes.

Meanwhile, brown the slices of pork in batches in a hot, nonstick frying pan over medium-high heat, then drain them on paper towels. Add the pork to the casserole, cover, and simmer for 25 minutes, stirring occasionally, until the meat is tender. If using fresh peas, add these after the pork has been cooking for five minutes; if using frozen peas, add these after 20 minutes. Add the yellow pepper after 20 minutes. Just before serving, stir in the remaining chopped herbs.

SUGGESTED ACCOMPANIMENTS: *brown rice; green salad.*

Pork Vindaloo

Serves 8

Working time: about 15 minutes
Total time: about 1 day (includes marinating)

Calories **200**
Protein **22g.**
Cholesterol **70mg.**
Total fat **10g.**
Saturated fat **3g.**
Sodium **265mg.**

2 lb. lean leg or shoulder of pork, trimmed of fat and cut into small cubes
¾ lb. tomatoes, coarsely chopped
1 green pepper, seeded and chopped
1 large onion, sliced
3 garlic cloves, crushed
1 tbsp. safflower oil
1 tsp. cumin seeds
1 tsp. yellow mustard seeds
1 tsp. ground cinnamon
1 tsp. dry mustard
½ tsp. ground turmeric
10 black peppercorns, crushed
6 small red chili peppers, fresh or dried (caution, page 36)
6 tbsp. vinegar
2 tbsp. plain low-fat yogurt
½ lemon, grated zest and juice
¼ tsp. salt (optional)
4 tbsp. chopped cilantro

Heap all the ingredients except for the salt and cilantro in a large, nonreactive bowl, and using two spoons, gently toss them until they are well combined. Cover the bowl and set the mixture aside to marinate in the refrigerator for 24 hours. Transfer the contents of the bowl to a large saucepan, and simmer gently for one and a half hours, stirring occasionally and adding a little water if the mixture appears too dry. At the end of the cooking time, add the salt if desired. Stir in the chopped cilantro before serving.

SUGGESTED ACCOMPANIMENT: *mashed potatoes with cinnamon.*

EDITOR'S NOTE: *This dish will taste even better if kept in the refrigerator and eaten the next day.*

Red Pork

Serves 4
Working time: about 25 minutes
Total time: about 1 hour and 25 minutes (includes marinating)

Calories **235**
Protein **22g.**
Cholesterol **70mg.**
Total fat **15g.**
Saturated fat **4g.**
Sodium **180mg.**

1 lb. lean leg or shoulder of pork, trimmed of fat and cut into small cubes
1 lemon, juice only
2 tbsp. safflower oil
1 onion, very finely chopped
3 garlic cloves, crushed
6 large ripe tomatoes, finely chopped
1 tbsp. tomato paste
1 tsp. ground turmeric
8 black peppercorns, crushed
¼ tsp. coriander seeds, crushed
¼ tsp. salt
8 sprigs chopped cilantro

Put the pork into a shallow, nonreactive dish with the lemon juice and set it aside to marinate at room temperature for one hour.

Heat the oil in a frying pan, and add the onion, garlic, tomatoes, and tomato paste. Cook for three minutes, then add the turmeric, peppercorns, and pork, and cook, uncovered, for three minutes more to brown the pork. To prevent burning, you may need to add about 3 tablespoons of water. Add the coriander seeds and salt, cover the pan, and cook over medium heat until the meat is tender—about 15 minutes.

Serve the pork in a warmed dish garnished with the chopped cilantro.

SUGGESTED ACCOMPANIMENT: *a salad of chicory and orange segments, dressed with vinaigrette and topped with chives and orange zest.*

Pork Dopiaza

DOPIAZA, THE INDIAN TITLE OF THIS DISH, INDICATES THAT IT
CONTAINS TWICE THE AMOUNT OF ONIONS AS MEAT.

Serves 6
Working time: about 25 minutes
Total time: about 1 hour and 15 minutes

Calories **290**
Protein **27g.**
Cholesterol **80mg.**
Total fat **12g.**
Saturated fat **4g.**
Sodium **250mg.**

1½ lb. lean leg or shoulder of pork, trimmed of fat and cut into small cubes
4 tbsp. safflower oil
3 lb. onions, 2 lb. finely sliced, 1 lb. coarsely chopped
¾ lb. tomatoes, chopped
4 garlic cloves, crushed
1 tsp. ground coriander
1 tsp. chili powder
1 tsp. ground cinnamon
4 bay leaves
ground turmeric
2-inch piece fresh ginger, peeled and sliced
8 black peppercorns, crushed
1 tbsp. plain low-fat yogurt
½ tsp. salt
1 lemon, juice only
6 sprigs cilantro, torn into small pieces

Heat half of the oil in a large frying pan over medium-low heat, and add the pork, half the sliced onions, the tomatoes, garlic, ground coriander, chili powder, cinnamon, bay leaves, and about ½ teaspoon of turmeric. Toss the contents of the pan and cook for two minutes, stirring occasionally. Add the remaining sliced onions, cover the pan, and cook over low heat for one hour, or until tender.

About 15 minutes before serving, heat the remaining oil in another pan, and add the chopped onions, the ginger, peppercorns, and a pinch of turmeric for color. Cook until the onions are nearly golden, then stir in the yogurt. Add the contents of the second pan to the first, and season with the salt and lemon juice. Serve in the pan, garnished with the cilantro.

SUGGESTED ACCOMPANIMENT: *plain boiled rice.*

Vinegar Pork with Garlic

Serves 6
Working time: about 20 minutes
Total time: about 1 hour and 40 minutes (includes marinating)

Calories **300**
Protein **33g.**
Cholesterol **80mg.**
Total fat **13g.**
Saturated fat **5g.**
Sodium **130mg.**

2 lb. boned leg of pork, trimmed of fat and cut into 1½-inch cubes
3 tbsp. low-sodium soy sauce
5 tbsp. clear vinegar
2 tbsp. safflower oil
1 head of garlic (about 12 cloves), cloves peeled and quartered
1 tsp. black peppercorns, coarsely crushed
¾ lb. waxy potatoes, quartered

Sprinkle the meat with the soy sauce and vinegar; let it marinate at room temperature for at least 30 minutes. Heat the oil in a large, flameproof casserole over high heat. Add the garlic and stir for a few seconds, then lower the heat and spoon in the meat, reserving the marinade. Turn the meat in the oil for two to three minutes, until it no longer looks raw—do not let it brown. Add the peppercorns, the reserved marinade, the potatoes, and enough water to cover. Bring to a boil, cover, and simmer for 30 minutes.

Remove the lid and increase the heat. Continue cooking for another 20 to 30 minutes, stirring often, until the meat is tender and coated with a thick sauce.

SUGGESTED ACCOMPANIMENTS: *boiled rice or sweet potatoes; sautéed okra.*

Pork Schpundra

IN THIS LIGHT VERSION OF SCHPUNDRA, AN EASTERN EUROPEAN
CASSEROLE WITH BEETS, THE TRADITIONAL LIQUOR KNOWN AS
KVASS IS REPLACED WITH BEER, YOGURT, AND MINT.

Serves 4
Working time: about 20 minutes
Total time: about 1 hour and 20 minutes

Calories **240**
Protein **25g.**
Cholesterol **70mg.**
Total fat **8g.**
Saturated fat **3g.**
Sodium **400mg.**

1 lb. lean stewing pork, trimmed of fat and cut into ¾-inch cubes
1 tbsp. safflower oil
1 lb. fresh beets, peeled and cut into ¾-inch cubes
1 red onion, sliced
1½ cups light beer
1 tbsp. molasses
8 black peppercorns
4 allspice berries
1 fresh or dried bay leaf
1 sprig fresh mint
½ tsp. salt
1 tbsp. cornstarch, dissolved in 2 tbsp. water
½ cup plain low-fat yogurt

Heat the oil in a large, flameproof casserole over high
heat. Add the meat and cook until it is browned evenly
on all sides—about one minute. Add the beets, onion,
beer, molasses, peppercorns, allspice, bay leaf, mint,
and salt. Bring to a boil and simmer gently for one to
one and a quarter hours, until the meat is tender.

Add the cornstarch mixture to the casserole and
cook for a few minutes more to thicken the liquid,
stirring all the time. Serve hot, topping each serving
with a swirl of the yogurt.

SUGGESTED ACCOMPANIMENT: *rye bread.*

Mexican Pork

Serves 4
Working time: about 20 minutes
Total time: about 8 hours (includes soaking)

Calories **250**
Protein **25g.**
Cholesterol **80mg.**
Total fat **11g.**
Saturated fat **4g.**
Sodium **290mg.**

1 lb. pork tenderloin, trimmed of fat and cut into 1-inch cubes
⅓ cup dried kidney beans, soaked in cold water for 7 to 8 hours, or overnight
1 tbsp. virgin olive oil
1 onion, finely chopped
1 garlic clove, crushed
1 tsp. chili powder
¼ tsp. ground allspice
1½ tbsp. tomato paste
1¼ cups unsalted chicken stock (recipe, page 139)
2 tsp. arrowroot
½ tsp. salt
2 tbsp. sour cream
2 tbsp. plain low-fat yogurt

Drain the beans, place them in a pan, cover with water, and bring to a boil. Boil rapidly for at least 10 minutes, then lower the heat, cover, and simmer until the beans are tender—25 to 30 minutes. Drain well.

Heat the oil in a large, heavy-bottomed pan on medium high; add the pork, onion, and garlic; cook for about five minutes, stirring frequently to brown the meat all over. Stir in the chili powder, allspice, and tomato paste; add the stock. Bring to a boil, then lower the heat, cover, and simmer for 20 minutes.

Add the cooked kidney beans to the pan. In a small bowl, mix the arrowroot with 2 tablespoons of cold water. Add the arrowroot mixture to the pan and stir well, until the juices thicken. Season with the salt.

Mix together the sour cream and yogurt. Spoon one-quarter of the mixture onto each serving.

Red-Pepper Pork with Mint

Serves 4
Working (and total) time: about 35 minutes

Calories **220**
Protein **24g.**
Cholesterol **70mg.**
Total fat **12g.**
Saturated fat **3g.**
Sodium **90mg.**

1 lb. pork tenderloin or loin, trimmed of fat and thinly sliced
1 tbsp. virgin olive oil
2 sweet red peppers, quartered, seeded, deribbed, and thinly sliced
freshly ground black pepper
1 lb. tomatoes, peeled, seeded, and roughly chopped
¼ tsp. salt
2 tbsp. finely chopped fresh mint
¼ cup plain low-fat yogurt (optional)

Heat the oil in a heavy-bottomed skillet over high heat; add the red peppers and sauté them for one minute. Add the pork slices and sauté them for several minutes, turning them to brown both sides. Season with some pepper, cover, and lower the heat. After five minutes, add the tomatoes; continue to cook, covered, until the meat is tender and the tomato-pepper mixture is reduced—10 to 15 minutes. Season with the salt and some more pepper if desired.

Remove the pan from the heat and let it cool for one minute, then stir in the mint and the yogurt, if you are using it. Serve at once.

SUGGESTED ACCOMPANIMENTS: *rice, pasta, or new potatoes; crusty bread; green salad.*

Tenderloin in Red Wine with Prunes

Serves 4
Working time: about 20 minutes
Total time: about 1 hour and 20 minutes

Calories **215**
Protein **23g.**
Cholesterol **70mg.**
Total fat **12g.**
Saturated fat **4g.**
Sodium **280mg.**

1 lb. pork tenderloin, trimmed of fat and cut crosswise into ½-inch-thick slices
1 tbsp. virgin olive oil
1 onion, sliced
½ lb. button mushrooms, quartered if large
1½ cups Beaujolais or other fruity red wine
8 large ready-to-eat prunes
1 bay leaf
½ tsp. salt
freshly ground black pepper
1 tsp. cornstarch mixed with 1 tbsp. water
⅓ cup plain low-fat yogurt

Preheat the oven to 350° F.

Heat half of the olive oil in a nonstick frying pan over high heat and brown the slices of pork on both sides—one to two minutes per side. As each of the slices becomes brown, transfer it to a flameproof casserole.

Add the remaining oil to the pan and lower the heat to medium high. Add the onion and mushrooms, and cook, stirring, until they are browned—about five minutes. Add the vegetables to the casserole.

Pour the wine into the frying pan and bring it to a boil, stirring to mix in any browned bits on the bottom of the pan. Pour the wine into the casserole, and add the prunes, bay leaf, salt, and some pepper. Cover the casserole tightly and cook in the oven for one hour.

Using a slotted spoon, transfer the pork, prunes, and vegetables to a heated serving dish; keep the food hot in a low oven. Remove the bay leaf from the casserole and discard it. Add the cornstarch mixture to the cooking liquid, stirring well. Bring to a boil, stirring until the sauce is smooth and thickened. Remove the casserole from the heat and stir in the yogurt.

Pour the sauce over the pork and mix it in gently. Serve immediately.

EDITOR'S NOTE: *The prunes used in this recipe are sold for eating straight from the package and do not require presoaking or pitting. If you use ordinary dried prunes, soak them in cold water for three hours and pit them before cooking.*

Coachman's Pork

IN THIS VERSION OF A SCANDINAVIAN DISH, THE MEAT AND
ONIONS ARE BROWNED IN A LITTLE OIL INSTEAD OF BUTTER.

Serves 6
Working time: about 40 minutes
Total time: about 2 hours and 40 minutes

Calories **235**
Protein **19g.**
Cholesterol **125mg.**
Total fat **7g.**
Saturated fat **3g.**
Sodium **280mg.**

1 lb. pork loin or other lean pork, cut into strips about ½ inch by 2 inches
2 tsp. safflower oil
1½ lb. onions, thickly sliced
4 lamb's kidneys, quartered and trimmed
2 lb. potatoes, cut into ⅛-inch slices
¾ cup beer
1¼ cups unsalted veal stock (recipe, page 139)
½ tsp. salt
freshly ground black pepper

Heat the oil in a frying pan on medium. Add the onions and cook, stirring occasionally, until the onions start browning at the edges. Remove them from the pan and set them aside. In the same pan, fry the pork strips, a few at a time, until they are well browned; remove the pork from the pan and set it aside. Fry the kidney pieces in the pan for several minutes to sear them.

Preheat the oven to 375° F. In the bottom of a deep, ovenproof dish, spread one-third of the onions, then one-third of the potatoes, the kidneys, another third of the onions, another third of the potatoes, the pork, then a final layer of onions topped with potatoes.

Over high heat, deglaze the frying pan with the beer. Boil rapidly until the beer is almost completely evaporated; add the stock and bring the mixture back to a boil. Add the salt and some pepper, and pour the liquid over the ingredients in the dish. Cover the dish with foil and bake for two hours, removing the foil after the first hour to brown the top. Serve hot.

SUGGESTED ACCOMPANIMENT: *steamed winter greens.*

Tenderloin with Rice and Vegetables

THIS MILD VERSION OF JAMBALAYA PROVIDES AN
APPETIZING MEAL FOR THE ENTIRE FAMILY.

Serves 4
Working time: about 30 minutes
Total time: about 1 hour and 20 minutes

Calories **565**
Protein **34g.**
Cholesterol **70mg.**
Total fat **15g.**
Saturated fat **4g.**
Sodium **330mg.**

1 lb. pork tenderloin, trimmed of fat and cubed
2 tbsp. safflower oil
1 onion, chopped
1 large garlic clove, finely chopped
1 lb. ripe tomatoes, peeled and chopped, or 14 oz. canned whole tomatoes, chopped
2 cups pureed tomatoes
1 tsp. mild chili powder
1 tbsp. Worcestershire sauce
cayenne pepper
½ tsp. salt
freshly ground black pepper
hot red-pepper sauce
1 green pepper, seeded, deribbed, and diced
2 ribs celery, diced
1 eggplant, (about ½ lb.), cubed
½ lb. zucchini, cubed
1¼ cups long-grain rice

Heat 1 tablespoon of the oil in a large, flameproof casserole over high heat. Add the pork cubes and cook for two minutes, stirring all the time. Stir in the onion and garlic, and cook for one minute more.

Add the chopped tomatoes, pureed tomatoes, chili powder, Worcestershire sauce, a pinch of cayenne pepper, the salt, some freshly ground black pepper, and a few drops of hot red-pepper sauce, and stir well. Cover and cook over low heat for 20 minutes, stirring from time to time.

In the meantime, heat the remaining safflower oil in a frying pan over medium heat. Add the green pepper, celery, and eggplant. Cook over low heat for five minutes, then stir in the zucchini and cook for another five minutes.

Add the rice and vegetables to the meat in the casserole, and stir to combine them. Cover again and continue cooking until the rice is tender and all the excess liquid has been absorbed—10 to 15 minutes. Depending on how much liquid the vegetables exude, you may need to add a little water from time to time. Fluff up the rice with a fork and serve hot.

SUGGESTED ACCOMPANIMENT: *tossed green salad.*

Blanquette Anisette

IN THIS VERSION OF A TRADITIONAL BLANQUETTE—A VEAL STEW
IN A WHITE SAUCE—THE SAUCE IS MADE WITH SKIM MILK AND
YOGURT INSTEAD OF EGGS AND CREAM. THE FENNEL AND THE
LIQUEUR CONTRIBUTE TO THE DISTINCTIVE ANISE FLAVOR.

Serves 4
Working time: about 40 minutes
Total time: about 1 hour and 40 minutes

Calories **250**
Protein **25g.**
Cholesterol **100mg.**
Total fat **8g.**
Saturated fat **3g.**
Sodium **370mg.**

1 lb. lean pork for stewing, trimmed of fat and diced
3 cups unsalted chicken stock (recipe, page 139) or water
1 fennel bulb, feathery top reserved
1 clove (optional)
1 bay leaf, fresh or dried
3 shallots, peeled and separated (optional)
4 oz. white button mushrooms
⅔ cup dry white wine
1 to 2 tbsp. fresh lemon juice
½ lb. white baby turnips, or larger turnips, halved or quartered
½ tsp. salt
⅔ cup skim milk
½ tsp. cornstarch
1 egg yolk
4 tbsp. plain low-fat yogurt
1 tbsp. anise-flavored liqueur (optional)

Put the pork into a large casserole and add the stock
or water; the liquid should cover the meat. Bring to a
boil slowly and skim the surface before adding the
fennel bulb—studded with the clove, if you are using
it—the bay leaf, and the shallots, if you are using them.

Simmer very gently, skimming occasionally, for
about one hour, or until the meat is nearly tender.
Cook the mushrooms for a minute or two in the wine,
with a dash of lemon juice added to preserve their
whiteness. Place them in the casserole with the cooking liquid, and add the turnips and the salt. Simmer for
20 minutes more. Test the vegetables for tenderness
and drain the contents of the casserole, reserving the
cooking liquid. Discard the clove, bay leaf, and the
shallots, if used. Cut the fennel bulb into quarters or
pieces about the same size as the other vegetables.

Strain the cooking liquid through a fine sieve into a
measuring bowl. Reserve 1 tablespoon of the milk, and
add the cooking liquid to the remaining milk to make
2 cups. Combine the cornstarch with the reserved
milk, and beat together with the egg yolk and yogurt.
Beat a little of the stock-and-milk liquid into the egg
mixture, then whisk the mixture into the rest of the
stock; return the stock to the casserole and bring it to
a simmer, stirring or whisking all the time.

Return the pork and vegetables to the casserole and
continue heating the contents over very low heat until
the liquid coats the back of a spoon; do not let the
liquid boil, or it may curdle. Remove the casserole from
the heat, stir in the liqueur, if you are using it, and add
the remaining lemon juice to taste. Chop the reserved
fennel and scatter it over the top before serving.

Frikadeller Pork

FRIKADELLER ARE SCANDINAVIAN MEATBALLS MADE WITH LEAN PORK AND VEAL. IN THIS RECIPE, THE AMOUNT OF CALORIES PER PORTION IS KEPT VERY LOW BY COMBINING THE MEAT WITH FRESH VEGETABLES.

Serves 8
Working (and total) time: about 1 hour

Calories **112**
Protein **17g.**
Cholesterol **62mg.**
Total fat **4g.**
Saturated fat **3g.**
Sodium **206mg.**

¾ lb. lean pork
¾ lb. lean veal
1½ tbsp. cornstarch
1 cup club soda, or 1 tsp. baking soda dissolved in 1 cup water
1 onion, finely chopped
1½ tsp. ground caraway seeds
¾ tsp. salt
1½ tbsp. kümmel (optional)
½ lb. broccoli florets
½ lb. cauliflower florets
½ lb. small carrots
½ lb. kohlrabi or small turnips
6 cups unsalted vegetable stock (recipe, page 139)
1 small bunch parsley or carrot tops, finely chopped

Chop the pork and veal in a food processor until they are smooth, or put the meats through a grinder three times. Beat the cornstarch and club soda or baking-soda mixture into the meat until the mixture is almost fluffy in appearance; mix in the onion, caraway seeds, salt, and the kümmel, if you are using it. Let the mixture chill in the refrigerator.

Cut the broccoli, cauliflower, carrots, and kohlrabi or turnips into approximately equal-size pieces, about 1 inch across; leave the root vegetables whole if they are sufficiently young and small. Divide the stock between two large cooking pots and bring both to a boil.

To cook the frikadeller, drop teaspoons of the meat mixture into one pot of simmering stock. You will have at least three dozen little dumplings, and since they expand considerably during cooking, it will be necessary to poach them in batches. Poach each batch at a gentle simmer for five to seven minutes, turning occasionally with a slotted spoon (the frikadeller are not necessarily cooked through when they rise to the surface of the liquid). Replenish the liquid in the pan with hot water as the stock evaporates. Remove each batch of cooked frikadeller with a slotted spoon and keep it warm in a colander placed over the second pot.

While poaching the last batch of frikadeller, cook the vegetables in the second pot of simmering stock. Drain them when they are done—they should be just tender—and reserve the stock. Once all the frikadeller and the vegetables are cooked, combine the cooking liquids and strain through a fine sieve. Return the liquid to a simmer in a flameproof casserole or one of the pots already used, and add all the frikadeller and vegetables. Warm through briefly and scatter with the chopped parsley or carrot tops before serving.

Wine and Vegetable Pork

Serves 4
Working time: about 30 minutes
Total time: about 45 minutes

Calories **300**
Protein **24g.**
Cholesterol **75mg.**
Total fat **15g.**
Saturated fat **5g.**
Sodium **310mg.**

1 lb. pork tenderloin, trimmed of fat and cut into 1½-inch strips
freshly ground black pepper
2 tbsp. virgin olive oil
1 large onion, chopped
2 carrots, sliced into rounds
1 leek, white part only, sliced into rounds
1 cup white wine
½ cup unsalted vegetable stock (recipe, page 139)
1 tbsp. finely chopped fresh thyme, or 1 tsp. dried thyme leaves
1 tbsp. finely chopped fresh rosemary, or 1 tsp. dried rosemary
1 bay leaf
½ lb. tomatoes
½ lb. snow peas, strings removed
1 tbsp. light cream (optional)
½ tsp. salt
4 tbsp. chopped parsley

Sprinkle some black pepper over the pork strips and rub it in with the tips of your fingers. Heat the oil in a nonstick, flameproof casserole over high heat until it is hot but not smoking, then add the pork and stir vigorously. When the meat is browned on both sides—about two minutes—remove it and keep it warm.

Lower the heat and add the onion, carrots, and leek to the casserole. Cook over low heat until the vegetables soften—about three minutes. Add the wine, stock, thyme, rosemary, and bay leaf, and bring to a boil. Simmer for 10 minutes, stirring occasionally.

Meanwhile, core the tomatoes and cut a small cross in the skin on the bottom of each, then plunge them into boiling water for 10 seconds. Remove the tomatoes and refresh them in cold water. Peel off the skin in sections, starting at the bottom of each tomato and working toward the stem end; cut the tomatoes into slivers and press out the seeds. Put the snow peas into a pan of boiling water and cook until they are soft but still crunchy—about two minutes. Drain and refresh under cold running water.

Return the meat to the casserole along with any juices that have collected in the dish, and cook over low heat for five minutes. Add the cream, if you are using it, and the salt, and stir. After one minute, add the snow peas, tomatoes, and 3 tablespoons of the parsley, and warm through quickly. Transfer the contents of the pan to a warmed serving dish, sprinkle with the remaining parsley, and serve immediately.

SUGGESTED ACCOMPANIMENT: *plain boiled rice.*

EDITOR'S NOTE: *Instead of snow peas, 6 ounces of trimmed green beans may be used in this recipe.*

Pork with Wheat Berries and Gin

Serves 4
Working time: about 20 minutes
Total time: about 10 hours (includes soaking)

Calories **280**
Protein **24g.**
Cholesterol **60mg.**
Total fat **8g.**
Saturated fat **3g.**
Sodium **75mg.**

¾ lb. pork tenderloin, cut into strips about ½ inch by 2 inches
½ cup whole wheat berries
1 orange, peeled and divided into segments, 1 strip of zest pared and reserved
10 juniper berries, crushed
¾ cup fresh orange juice
3 tbsp. gin
½ cup thinly sliced scallions
¼ cup plain low-fat yogurt
1 tbsp. chopped parsley
freshly ground black pepper

Place the wheat berries and the orange zest in a saucepan of cold water, and let them soak overnight. Drain the wheat, add it to a pan of boiling water, and simmer until the kernels are just tender—about 45 minutes.

While the wheat berries are cooking, heat the juniper berries in a small, heavy-bottomed saucepan over medium heat for about three minutes, then add the orange juice and gin. Warm through over low heat, then cover, remove from the heat, and let them infuse for 30 minutes.

Heat the juniper infusion to just below the simmering point. Add the pork in two or three batches and poach each batch for two minutes; lift each batch from the liquid with a slotted spoon when it is cooked, and keep it warm. Add the scallions to the liquid, then simmer until the liquid is reduced by one-third and the scallions are cooked. Add any juices from the pork toward the end of the cooking time. Reduce the heat to very low and whisk in the yogurt.

When the kernels are cooked, drain them and place them in a warmed serving bowl, discarding the orange zest. Remove the sauce from the heat; add the pork, parsley, and some pepper. Pour the sauce over the wheat berries and toss with the orange segments.

Fennel Pork

Serves 6
Working (and total) time: about 40 minutes

Calories **160**
Protein **22g.**
Cholesterol **70mg.**
Total fat **7g.**
Saturated fat **3g.**
Sodium **220mg.**

6 boned pork steaks (about 4 oz. each), trimmed of fat
freshly ground black pepper
¾ lb. fennel bulbs, feathery tops reserved for garnish
1½ cups unsalted veal or chicken stock (recipes, page 139)
1 tbsp. anise-flavored liqueur
¼ cup plain low-fat yogurt
¼ tsp. salt
ground white pepper

Using a small, sharp knife, cut into the side of each steak to make a deep pocket *(page 12, Step 3)*. Season the pockets with some black pepper. Remove three outer leaves from each of the fennel bulbs and cut each leaf in half. In a large saucepan, simmer the leaves in the stock for five minutes. Lift the fennel from the stock with a slotted spoon and divide it among the pockets in the steaks. Place the meat in a steamer.

Chop the remaining fennel and add it to the stock. Place the steamer over the stock and steam the steaks until their juices run clear when pierced, turning them over halfway through—six to eight minutes. Remove the steamer from the pan and keep the steaks warm.

Continue to boil the fennel in the stock until it is tender—about five minutes—then remove it with a slotted spoon and set it aside. Add the liqueur to the stock and boil until the liquid has reduced to about 4 tablespoons, then put it into a food processor with the fennel and yogurt, and puree the ingredients. Transfer the puree to a saucepan, add the salt and some white pepper, and warm over low heat, stirring occasionally.

Place the steaks on a warmed serving dish, spoon the sauce around them, and garnish with the fennel.

SUGGESTED ACCOMPANIMENT: *green beans.*

Pork Couscous

Serves 6
Working time: about 30 minutes
Total time: about 1 hour and 30 minutes
(includes marinating)

Calories **400**
Protein **25g.**
Cholesterol **80mg.**
Total fat **15g.**
Saturated fat **5g.**
Sodium **380mg.**

1½ lb. lean pork, trimmed of fat and cut into ½-inch cubes
1 onion
1 lemon, juice only
1 tsp. salt
½ tsp. ground cinnamon
2-inch piece fresh ginger
6 small turnips, or chunks of large turnips
6 small carrots, or chunks of large carrots
¾ lb. eggplant cut into 1-inch cubes
¾ lb. small zucchini, sliced diagonally
6 fresh or dried dates, pitted and halved
¾ cup cooked chick-peas
1 lb. couscous (about 2½ cups)
1½ tbsp. Harissa or other hot-pepper sauce

Puree the onion with the lemon juice, salt, and cinnamon in a food processor; alternatively, grate the onion finely, then mix it with the other three ingredients. Marinate the pork in this paste for 30 minutes.

Place the piece of ginger in 2 cups of water in a saucepan over which you can put a closely fitting two-tier steamer with a lid. Bring the water to a boil.

Pick out the pieces of meat from the marinade, but do not scrape off any of the paste that sticks to them. Arrange the meat in the bottom tier of the steamer with the turnips, carrots, and eggplant. Set this, covered, over the boiling water and let it steam for 30 minutes. Check from time to time that the water has not boiled away.

Add the zucchini, dates, and chick-peas to the meat mixture. Cover and steam for 20 minutes more.

Meanwhile, put the couscous into a large bowl. Pour 2 cups of lukewarm water over the couscous and let it swell for 10 minutes, stirring occasionally to prevent lumps from forming.

About 10 minutes before the meat and vegetables are ready, put the couscous into the upper tier of the steamer to heat through uncovered. The couscous is done when the steam begins to penetrate its upper surface. If this has not happened by the time the meat and vegetables are cooked, take out the bottom tier and put the couscous directly over the saucepan.

Pile the couscous onto a serving platter, and top it with the meat and vegetables. Dilute the Harissa with about 1 cup of the hot, gingery steaming liquid, and serve it separately. The remaining liquid may also be passed around at the table separately to moisten the meat and vegetables.

Pork and Bulgur Meatballs

Serves 6
Working time: about 30 minutes
Total time: about 1 hour and 10 minutes

Calories **240**
Protein **27g.**
Cholesterol **70mg.**
Total fat **9g.**
Saturated fat **5g.**
Sodium **230mg.**

1½ lb. lean pork, ground or very finely chopped
⅔ cup fine-grade bulgur
3 tbsp. very finely chopped onion
¾ tsp. ground roasted cumin seed
½ tsp. salt
freshly ground black pepper
4 tbsp. finely chopped parsley
½ cup sour half-and-half
1 tsp. arrowroot
1 garlic clove, finely chopped
½ tsp. grated lemon zest
cayenne pepper

Knead the pork with the bulgur, onion, cumin, salt, and some pepper. Let the mixture stand for 10 minutes, knead again briefly, then form the mixture into 24 balls. Roll the balls in the parsley, pressing them in so that the herb coating sticks. Arrange the balls, in a single layer, in a steamer over a saucepan of boiling water, cover, and steam for 40 minutes.

Toward the end of this time, put the sour half-and-half into a pan. Mix the arrowroot with 1 teaspoon of cold water and stir this mixture into the half-and-half; add the garlic, the lemon zest, and a pinch of cayenne. Gradually beat in 6 tablespoons of hot water from the steaming pan and bring the sauce to a boil over medium heat, stirring constantly. When the sauce has thickened, remove it from the heat and let it stand for five minutes to absorb the arrowroot. Bring the sauce back to a boil just before serving. Serve the meatballs directly from the steamer, accompanied by the sauce.

EDITOR'S NOTE: *A bamboo steamer will provide a wider and flatter surface for the meatballs than an ordinary steamer.*

3 *Thinly sliced pork, mushrooms, daikon radish, shrimp, and other ingredients stand ready to be folded inside moistened rice-paper wrappers (recipe, page 102).*

Dishes with an Unusual Twist

No meat is more versatile than pork, and the recipes in this chapter offer many variations on the basic cooking methods encompassed in the previous two. The diverse collection of dishes that follows demonstrates that the need to control fat levels and calories can be a spur to invention rather than a handicap.

Some of the recipes are meant to be served cold. Such dishes as pork and spinach terrine *(page 101)*, pork salad with mustard vinaigrette *(page 118)*, and stuffed pig's feet *(page 117)* derive their inspiration from the French charcuterie—a shop that sells cooked pork products. Traditional charcuterie dishes were a means of using up the pig's abundant fat, which, unlike that of beef and lamb, is very palatable when cold. But this chapter's charcuterie is prepared with ingredients and cooking techniques that keep the fat level within reasonable bounds.

Other recipes in the chapter extend the meat with a satisfying complement of pastry, potatoes, bread, beans, or rice. An international selection of rice dishes includes an Italian risotto flavored with Parmesan cheese *(page 106)*, a Turkish pilaf with pine nuts and currants *(page 107)*, and a Dutch-Indonesian *nasi goreng (page 104)*, in which shrimp and omelette slices complement the pork.

Another group of recipes features pork presented in edible wrappers. Pork stuffings are enclosed in ravioli *(page 112)*, manicotti *(page 120)*, phyllo pastry *(page 119)*, Nappa cabbage leaves *(page 103)*, and rice-paper wrappers *(opposite)*. Conversely, thin slices of lean pork or pork kidneys are themselves used as containers for a vegetable filling *(page 109)*.

The recipes for stuffings and meatballs in this chapter frequently call for lean ground pork. To avoid the excessive fat content of the ground pork usually available, you can either order lean ground pork specially from your butcher or buy a lean cut of pork and grind or finely chop it yourself. The technique for finely chopping meat by hand is demonstrated on page 11.

Ham with Fava Beans

Serves 6
Working time: about 15 minutes
Total time: about 30 minutes

Calories **130**
Protein **10g.**
Cholesterol **15mg.**
Total fat **4g.**
Saturated fat **2g.**
Sodium **390mg.**

6 oz. lean ham, diced
1½ lb. shelled fava beans
1 tsp. safflower oil
1 tbsp. all-purpose flour
4 tbsp. white wine (optional)
freshly ground black pepper
2 tbsp. light cream
2 tbsp. finely chopped fresh summer savory, or 1½ tsp. dried summer savory

Bring a saucepan of water to a boil, add the beans, and simmer until they are tender but still crisp—about five minutes. Drain them in a colander set over a bowl and set them aside, reserving the strained liquid.

Heat the oil in a large, heavy-bottomed saucepan over medium heat; add the ham and cook for one minute. Add the flour and cook for one minute more, stirring continuously. Add the wine, if you are using it, and about ⅔ cup of the reserved bean-cooking water. Simmer for two minutes, adding more water if the sauce is too thick. Season with some pepper. Add the cream and allow it to bubble up once. Stir the beans into the pan, allow them to warm through, sprinkle with the summer savory, and serve.

EDITOR'S NOTE: *The skin of fava beans is rich in fiber but has a slightly bitter taste; if preferred, the beans may be peeled before cooking.*

Pork and Spinach Terrine

Serves 12
Working time: about 45 minutes
Total time: about 11 hours (includes chilling)

Calories **135**
Protein **16g.**
Cholesterol **45mg.**
Total fat **5g.**
Saturated fat **2g.**
Sodium **190mg.**

1½ lb. lean pork, trimmed of fat and cut into cubes
1 large onion, finely chopped
1½ cups fresh whole-wheat bread crumbs
2 garlic cloves, crushed
1 egg, beaten
1 tbsp. virgin olive oil
1½ tsp. chopped fresh sage
½ tsp. salt
freshly ground black pepper
5 oz. boneless chicken breast, skinned
1 tbsp. dry vermouth
12 large spinach leaves, washed and trimmed
lemon slices for garnish

Chop the pork very finely in a food processor or by hand *(technique, page 11)*. Put the pork into a bowl, and add the onion, bread crumbs, garlic, egg, oil, sage, half the salt, and some pepper. Mix the ingredients together well and set aside.

Cut the chicken breast into thin slices, and place them in a bowl with the dry vermouth, the remaining salt, and some pepper. Reserve eight spinach leaves; finely shred the remainder, add them to the chicken slices, and mix well. Preheat the oven to 350° F.

Blanch the reserved spinach in a little boiling water in a saucepan for one minute. Drain the leaves and refresh them with cold water, then drain well again. Pat the leaves dry on paper towels. Use the spinach to line the bottom and sides of a 9-by-5-inch loaf pan: Arrange three leaves, slightly overlapping, on the bottom and along each side of the pan, and place the remaining leaves at either end of the pan. Allow the leaves' edges to overlap the rim of the pan.

Press half the pork mixture into the lined pan. Arrange the chicken slices over the pork, then top with the remaining pork mixture and press to level the surface. Fold the overlapping spinach over the mixture, then cover with lightly greased foil and place the loaf pan inside a roasting pan filled halfway with cold water. Cook in the oven for one and three quarter hours.

Remove the loaf pan from the oven, cover it with clean foil, and weight it down with a heavy weight placed on a small board or a lid that fits over the top of the terrine. Let the terrine cool, then chill it in the refrigerator for about eight hours. Turn the terrine out of the pan onto a serving board or a platter. Pat the terrine dry with paper towels and garnish with lemon slices. Serve sliced.

EDITOR'S NOTE: *Grape leaves may be used instead of spinach to line the loaf pan. Grape leaves preserved in brine should first be rinsed well to remove the salt.*

Vietnamese Spring Rolls

SPRING ROLLS ARE USUALLY DEEP FRIED, ADDING TO THEIR
CALORIE CONTENT. HERE, THE DEEP FRYING IS OMITTED,
RETAINING THE FRESHNESS OF THE FILLING AND THE WRAPPERS.

Serves 4 as a main course, 8 as a starter
Working time: about 45 minutes
Total time: about 1 hour and 30 minutes

Calories **235**
Protein **26g.**
Cholesterol **90mg.**
Total fat **11g.**
Saturated fat **3g.**
Sodium **140mg.**

¾ lb. pork tenderloin
2-inch piece fresh ginger, peeled and sliced
14 scallions, white parts only
3 tbsp. low-sodium soy sauce
1½ cups unsalted vegetable or chicken stock (recipes, page 139)
½ lb. daikon radish, peeled and cut into thin 1½-inch-long strips
1 tbsp. safflower oil
1 or 2 fresh green chili peppers, finely sliced (caution, page 36)
¼ lb. peeled shrimp
¾ oz. dried shiitake mushrooms, soaked in hot water for 20 minutes, drained, and thinly sliced
¾ cup bean sprouts
16 crisp romaine or iceberg lettuce leaves
16 rice-paper wrappers
¾ cup fresh basil or mint leaves

Put the pork into a heavy-bottomed saucepan, and
add the ginger, two of the scallions, 2 tablespoons of
the soy sauce, and 1 cup of the stock. Bring the liquid
to a boil, skim off any froth that rises to the surface,
then cover and simmer until the pork is tender—about
20 minutes. Remove the pan from the heat, then let
the pork cool in the liquid—about one hour.

Meanwhile, cook the daikon radish in the remaining
stock for one to two minutes to soften it. Drain the
daikon and set it aside.

To prepare the scallion brushes for the garnish,
make three or four 1-inch-long cuts through the tops

of the white stems of eight of the scallions. Put the scallions into a bowl of ice water and set them aside until the sliced tops have curled—about 30 minutes.

When the pork is cool, remove it from the liquid and slice it diagonally into thin strips. Finely chop the remaining scallions. Heat the oil in a wok or a deep, heavy-bottomed frying pan. Add the chopped scallions and chili peppers, and stir-fry over medium heat for one to two minutes to flavor the oil. Increase the heat, add the pork, daikon, shrimp, mushrooms, bean sprouts, and the remaining soy sauce, and stir-fry until the ingredients are combined and heated through—about three minutes. Remove from the heat.

Blanch the lettuce leaves in boiling water for 30 seconds, then remove the central vein of each leaf with a knife. Dip the wrappers one at a time in a bowl of tepid water and gently shake off any excess water.

Arrange the wrappers flat on a board and place one lettuce leaf in the center of each wrapper. Place a few basil or mint leaves on the lettuce, then a spoonful of the filling. Roll the wrappers up around the filling, tucking in the sides as you proceed. Arrange on individual plates and garnish with the scallion brushes. Serve cold.

SUGGESTED ACCOMPANIMENT: *a dipping sauce made with low-sodium soy sauce, crushed garlic, finely chopped chili pepper, and lemon juice.*

Stuffed Nappa Cabbage

Serves 6
Working (and total) time: about 1 hour

Calories **250**
Protein **27g.**
Cholesterol **90mg.**
Total fat **14g.**
Saturated fat **5g.**
Sodium **230mg.**

¾ lb. pork tenderloin, trimmed of fat and ground or very finely chopped
12 Nappa cabbage leaves
2 tbsp. safflower oil
1 onion, finely chopped
6 oz. brown cap or oyster mushrooms, chopped
2 oranges, juice and grated zest of 1½; pared, julienned zest of the other half
½ tsp. salt
freshly ground black pepper
½ tsp. grated nutmeg
1 tbsp. low-sodium soy sauce

Blanch the cabbage leaves for one minute and drain them flat on paper towels. Heat ½ tablespoon of the oil in a heavy skillet over medium-high heat. Add the onion and cook until it is translucent. Add the mushrooms and stir-fry for four to five minutes.

Mix the pork, onions, mushrooms, and grated orange zest; add the salt, some pepper, and the grated nutmeg. Pare down the thick parts of the stems of the cabbage leaves so they are flexible. Place about 1½ tablespoons of the pork mixture on the stem end of each leaf, then roll up the leaf and tuck in the sides.

Heat the remaining oil in the skillet and fry the parcels, seam side down, for about seven minutes, then turn and cook until golden—about seven minutes more. Transfer the parcels to a serving dish. Deglaze the pan with the soy sauce and the orange juice; reduce the liquid for a minute, then pour it over the parcels. Garnish with the orange julienne and serve.

Nasi Goreng

THIS VERSION OF A TRADITIONAL DUTCH INDONESIAN DISH,
WHICH IS USUALLY TOPPED WITH A SLICED FOUR-EGG OME-
LETTE, IS GARNISHED WITH ONE EGG. TO REDUCE THE
CHOLESTEROL CONTENT FURTHER, THE EGG MAY BE OMITTED.

Serves 6
Working time: about 25 minutes
Total time: about 1 hour and 15 minutes

Calories **350**
Protein **25g.**
Cholesterol **120mg.**
Total fat **12g.**
Saturated fat **3g.**
Sodium **125mg.**

¾ lb. pork tenderloin, trimmed of fat and cut into ½-inch cubes
1½ cups long-grain brown rice
2 tbsp. safflower oil
1 large onion, quartered and thinly sliced
1 garlic clove, chopped
1 green chili pepper, seeded, a few thin rings reserved for garnish, the remainder chopped (caution, page 36)
4 oz. boneless chicken breast, skinned and cut into ½-inch cubes
½ tsp. ground turmeric
½ tsp. paprika
¼ tsp. cayenne pepper
2 tbsp. low-sodium soy sauce
1 large tomato, peeled, seeded, and cut into thin slivers
6 oz. peeled cooked shrimp, deveined
Rolled omelette
1 egg
1 tsp. low-sodium soy sauce
1 tsp. safflower oil

Cook the brown rice in a large saucepan of boiling water, covered, until it is tender—approximately 40 minutes. Drain well, rinse under cold running water, and drain well again.

Heat the oil in a large frying pan over medium heat. Add the onion, garlic, and chopped chili pepper, and cook for three minutes, stirring frequently. Stir in the pork and chicken cubes, and cook for four minutes, stirring. Add the turmeric, paprika, and cayenne, and mix well, then stir in the rice and continue cooking for four minutes more, stirring constantly. Add the soy sauce, tomato, and half of the shrimp, and cook until heated through—about two minutes. Transfer the mixture to a warmed serving platter and keep it warm while you make the omelette.

In a bowl, beat the egg with the soy sauce. Heat the oil in a 6- to 7-inch frying pan over medium-low heat. Add the egg mixture and tilt the pan to cover the bottom evenly. Cook until the omelette is set—45 seconds to one minute. Loosen the omelette from the pan and turn it out onto a board, then roll up the omelette and cut it into thin slices.

Arrange the omelette slices around the base of the rice mixture or over the top. Garnish with the chili-pepper rings and the remaining shrimp.

Pork and Salsify Pie

Serves 6
Working time: about 1 hour
Total time: about 4 hours and 15 minutes
(includes marinating)

Calories **340**
Protein **17g.**
Cholesterol **65mg.**
Total fat **17g.**
Saturated fat **8g.**
Sodium **310mg.**

1 lb. lean pork for stewing, trimmed of fat and cut into 1-inch pieces
⅔ cup dry white wine
3 garlic cloves, crushed
1 small onion, quartered
2 fresh bay leaves
2 sprigs fresh thyme
¼ tsp. salt
freshly ground black pepper
½ lemon, juice only
½ lb. salsify
1 cup unsalted vegetable stock (recipe, page 139)
8 baby onions, peeled
¼ lb. tomatoes, peeled, seeded, and chopped
1 tbsp. capers, rinsed and chopped
½ tsp. green peppercorns in brine, drained and rinsed
1 tsp. arrowroot, mixed with 1 tsp. stock or water
Pastry dough
1½ cups unbleached all-purpose flour
¼ tsp. salt
1½ tbsp. unsalted butter, cut into small cubes
1½ tbsp. solid vegetable shortening, cut into cubes

Place the pork in a shallow, nonreactive dish; add the wine, garlic, onion, bay leaves, thyme, salt, and some pepper. Set the pork aside to marinate for two hours.

To make the pastry dough, first sift the flour and salt together into a bowl. Add the butter and shortening, and cut them into the flour with a pastry cutter or two knives until the mixture has a coarse, mealy texture. Sprinkle 1 to 2 tablespoons of water over the contents of the bowl and stir with a knife until the dough begins to cohere. Gather the dough into a ball, pressing it with your hands, wrap in plastic wrap or wax paper, and chill for 15 minutes before using.

Transfer the meat with its marinade to a saucepan, bring gently to a boil, and skim as necessary. Cover the pan and simmer the mixture gently for 30 minutes.

Meanwhile, add the lemon juice to a saucepan of water, then scrub and peel the salsify under running water, cut it into 1-inch lengths, and plunge these immediately into the acidulated water. Parboil the salsify until it is almost tender—about 20 minutes. Drain the salsify and reserve it.

Remove the meat from its cooking liquid. Discard the onion, garlic, and bay leaves, and add the stock to the cooking liquid. Return the meat to the pan with the salsify and baby onions, and simmer until the meat is nearly tender—about 30 minutes.

Preheat the oven to 375° F. Place a small, ovenproof funnel upside down in the center of a deep piedish; if you like, make a funnel out of aluminum foil. Remove the meat and vegetables from the saucepan, and arrange them in the dish with the tomatoes, capers, and peppercorns. Discard the thyme sprigs. Measure out 1¼ cups of cooking liquid (make up with additional stock, wine, or water if necessary). Blend the arrowroot mixture into the liquid and bring to a boil in a pan. Simmer the sauce gently for a minute or two until it is slightly thickened, then pour it into the piedish.

Roll out the pastry dough so that it will overlap the edges of the piedish by about 1 inch. Lift the dough onto the dish with the aid of a rolling pin, cutting a small slit to allow the funnel to protrude; fold the excess dough under itself to give a double thickness around the rim, and crimp the edges, pressing the pastry to the rim of the dish with your fingers. Place the dish in the oven and bake for 40 minutes. Serve hot.

Pork Risotto

Serves 4
Working time: about 25 minutes
Total time: about 40 minutes

Calories **460**
Protein **24g.**
Cholesterol **55mg.**
Total fat **12g.**
Saturated fat **4g.**
Sodium **100mg.**

¾ lb. pork tenderloin, trimmed of fat and cut into small cubes
1 tbsp. virgin olive oil
1 onion, finely chopped
1 garlic clove, crushed
4 oz. button mushrooms, coarsely chopped
½ tsp. chopped fresh sage
1½ cups Arborio rice
½ tsp. salt
freshly ground black pepper
1½ cups dry white wine
1 cup fresh peas, blanched in boiling water, or 1 cup frozen peas
1 tbsp. freshly grated Parmesan cheese
3 tbsp. flat-leaf parsley leaves, torn into small pieces

Heat the oil in a nonstick skillet, then add the cubes of meat and sauté them until they are brown—about 10 minutes. Stir in the onion and continue cooking until the onion begins to turn golden at the edges. Add the garlic, mushrooms, and sage. When the mushrooms soften, increase the heat, add the rice, salt, and some pepper, and stir for a couple of minutes.

Mix the white wine with an equal amount of water and pour half the liquid into the pan. Lower the heat and stir while bringing the mixture to a gentle simmer. Stir frequently until all of the liquid is absorbed—approximately 10 minutes.

Pour in the rest of the liquid and the peas, bring back to a simmer, and stir. Cover the pan and let the mixture cook very slowly, stirring from time to time, until the mixture is creamy but not mushy—10 to 15 minutes. Just before serving, stir in the cheese and parsley.

SUGGESTED ACCOMPANIMENT: *tomato salad.*

Pilaf with Pig's Heart

HEART IS RICH IN IRON, PROTEIN, AND B VITAMINS BUT HAS A
RELATIVELY HIGH CHOLESTEROL CONTENT. IT SHOULD BE
AVOIDED BY PERSONS WITH A HIGH CHOLESTEROL LEVEL.

Serves 6
Working time: about 20 minutes
Total time: about 45 minutes

Calories **565**
Protein **15g.**
Cholesterol **60mg.**
Total fat **15g.**
Saturated fat **3g.**
Sodium **175mg.**

1 pig's heart (about ½ lb.), trimmed of fat, finely diced
3 tbsp. virgin olive oil
1 onion, finely chopped
2 tbsp. pine nuts
2 cups long-grain rice
2 tbsp. currants
¼ tsp. sugar
¼ tsp. ground allspice
¼ tsp. ground cinnamon
½ tsp. salt
freshly ground black pepper
3 tbsp. finely chopped parsley

Heat the oil in a heavy-bottomed pan over medium heat and sauté the diced heart until it begins to brown—about five minutes. Add the onion and pine nuts, and cook until both are beginning to color. Add the rice and stir to coat well with oil, then stir in 3 cups of water, the currants, sugar, allspice, cinnamon, salt, and some pepper. Bring to a boil, lower the heat, cover, and simmer for 10 minutes. Stir in the parsley, re-cover the pan, and let the pilaf stand, off the heat, for 15 minutes more. Mix well and serve hot or warm.

SUGGESTED ACCOMPANIMENTS: *summer squash; ratatouille.*

Scandinavian Gratin

Serves 6
Working time: about 30 minutes
Total time: about 2 hours

Calories **290**
Protein **20g.**
Cholesterol **85mg.**
Total fat **13g.**
Saturated fat **4g.**
Sodium **365mg.**

½ lb. pork tenderloin or loin, trimmed of fat and cut into thin slices
1 lb. potatoes, thinly sliced
½ lb. onions, thinly sliced
¾ lb. fresh herring fillets
1 tsp. salt
ground white pepper
⅔ cup skim milk
1 egg yolk
½ cup plain low-fat yogurt
2 sprigs parsley, finely chopped (optional)

Preheat the oven to 425° F.

Lightly grease a 1½- to 2-quart baking dish. Layer the potatoes, onions, herring fillets, and pork in the dish, beginning and ending with a layer of potatoes and seasoning each layer lightly with the salt and some ground white pepper. Pour the skim milk over the contents of the casserole.

Place the dish in the center of the oven and bake for 15 minutes, then lower the oven temperature to 375° F. and bake the casserole for another hour. Check that the contents of the dish are tender by inserting a skewer in the center of the dish—it should meet with no resistance.

Remove the dish from the oven and carefully pour out the thin juices into a bowl. Beat the egg yolk with the low-fat yogurt, and beat a couple of spoonfuls of the hot cooking juices into the egg-yogurt mixture. Whisk this mixture into the remaining juices and pour the liquid over the contents cf the baking dish.

Return the dish to the oven for 15 minutes. If the top layer of potatoes is already browned, cover the dish for the first 10 minutes; if the potatoes still look a little pale at the end of the cooking time, brown them briefly under a broiler.

Serve hot, garnished with the chopped parsley, if you are using it.

SUGGESTED ACCOMPANIMENTS: *a colorful salad; green beans or garden peas.*

Italian "Money-Bags"

Serves 4
Working time: about 40 minutes
Total time: about 1 hour

Calories **200**
Protein **22g.**
Cholesterol **60mg.**
Total fat **10g.**
Saturated fat **4g.**
Sodium **340mg.**

¾ lb. pork tenderloin, trimmed of fat
½ tsp. salt
freshly ground black pepper
1 ear of corn, husked, or 4 oz. corn kernels
½ lb. broccoli
2 tsp. virgin olive oil
1 sweet red pepper, seeded, deribbed, and diced
¼ cup low-fat ricotta cheese
2 tbsp. fresh basil leaves, torn or chopped
1 tbsp. fresh oregano, chopped
1 oz. mozzarella

Cut the tenderloin into 20 rounds and pound these until they are almost translucent and three times their original size *(technique, page 12)*. Season with half of the salt and some freshly ground black pepper.

Cook the ear of corn in boiling water, covered, for seven minutes. Allow to cool a little, then slice off the kernels with a knife. Or, briefly blanch the corn kernels, if you are using them.

Separate the broccoli into at least 20 tiny florets; peel and dice the stalks. Blanch the broccoli briefly in boiling water and drain well.

Preheat the oven to 375° F. Brush the bottom and sides of a large, shallow, ovenproof dish with 1 teaspoon of the oil.

Mix the broccoli, corn, and red pepper with the ricotta and remaining salt, and add the basil and oregano. Divide this mixture equally among the 20 pieces of pork tenderloin. Gather up the edges of each piece to enclose the filling, leaving some of the vegetable stuffing exposed to view. Divide the mozzarella into 20 cubes and top each "money-bag" with a single cube of cheese. Add a little more ground black pepper to each open parcel and arrange the parcels in the ovenproof dish. Brush the remaining olive oil over the exposed surfaces of meat.

Bake the parcels in the center of the oven until the meat is cooked through and the edges are tinged brown—about 15 minutes. If you wish to brown the mozzarella topping a little more, place under a broiler for a moment, but do not allow the pork to stiffen too much. Serve hot.

SUGGESTED ACCOMPANIMENTS: *thin green and white noodles; crisp salad with a balsamic-vinegar dressing.*

Picnic Loaf

Serves 10
Working time: about 35 minutes
Total time: about 3 hours (includes chilling)

Calories **290**
Protein **13g.**
Cholesterol **70mg.**
Total fat **15g.**
Saturated fat **6g.**
Sodium **275mg.**

¾ lb. lean pork, ground or very finely chopped
⅔ cup brown rice
1 bunch scallions, chopped
2 eggs, hard cooked and chopped
2 tbsp. chopped fresh tarragon
2 tbsp. capers, rinsed and drained
8 green olives, pitted and coarsely chopped
1½ oz. anchovy fillets, rinsed and chopped
freshly ground black pepper
Flaky pastry
1⅔ cups all-purpose flour
½ tsp. salt
2 tbsp. unsalted butter, slightly softened
2 tbsp. solid vegetable shortening

To make the pastry dough, sift the flour and salt into a mixing bowl. Mix together the butter and vegetable shortening. Cut one-quarter of the butter and shortening mixture into the flour with a pastry cutter or two knives until the mixture resembles bread crumbs. Add just enough ice water to make the dough cohere, and continue to work the dough until it comes cleanly from the sides of the bowl. Shape the dough into a ball, wrap it in plastic wrap, and chill for 30 minutes. On a floured board, roll the dough into a rectangle about three times as long as it is wide. With a short side toward you, dot the top two-thirds of the rectangle with another quarter of the shortening mixture. Fold the bottom third over the center and the top third over that, and chill for 30 minutes. Roll out, dot with half of the remaining shortening mixture, fold, and chill.

Repeat the process one more time to work in all of the shortening mixture, then roll out the dough to make the final folds cohere. Wrap the dough in plastic wrap and refrigerate it until you are ready to use it.

Bring the rice to a boil in plenty of water and stir once. Cover and simmer for about 30 minutes or until cooked, then drain the rice in a sieve and rinse under cold running water. Let the rice cool in the sieve.

Brown the pork in a dry, nonstick frying pan over medium-high heat—about five minutes. Stir in the scallions and cook for another two minutes.

Preheat the oven to 425° F. Halve the pastry dough. Roll each piece into a thin sheet about 12 by 10 inches and place these on nonstick baking sheets.

Spread the rice onto each pastry sheet to within 1 inch of the ends, leaving about 3 inches of bare pastry on each side of the filling. Lay the meat mixture on top of the rice, and add the eggs, tarragon, capers, olives, and anchovies; make sure that each ingredient is evenly spread over the beds of rice. Add some pepper.

Brush the edges of the pastry with water, then bring the side flaps up and fold one over the other. Crimp the pastry along the center seam and at both ends to seal the loaves. Turn each loaf over so that the seam is underneath, and cut several slits in the pastry top to let steam escape. Bake the loaves until they are golden—about 15 minutes—then lower the oven temperature to 350° F. and cook for 20 minutes more.

Turn out the loaves onto a wire rack to cool. Transport the loaves whole; cut into thick slices to serve.

SUGGESTED ACCOMPANIMENTS: *a selection of salads.*

Pita Pork Balls

Serves 6
Working (and total) time: about 1 hour

Calories **230**
Protein **16g.**
Cholesterol **30mg.**
Total fat **6g.**
Saturated fat **2g.**
Sodium **280mg.**

½ lb. pork loin, trimmed of fat and ground or very finely chopped
¾ cup bulgur
2 tsp. safflower oil
1 onion, very finely chopped
1 garlic clove, crushed
2 tsp. curry powder
½ tsp. ground coriander
¼ tsp. ground cinnamon
¼ tsp. salt
6 whole wheat pita breads
8 romaine lettuce leaves, washed, dried, and shredded
4-inch piece cucumber, thinly sliced
½ lb. tomatoes, thinly sliced
Yogurt dressing
⅓ cup plain low-fat yogurt
1 tbsp. chopped fresh mint
1 tbsp. fresh lemon juice
cayenne pepper

Preheat the oven to 375° F. In a bowl, soak the bulgur in 1¼ cups of boiling water for 15 minutes to swell and absorb the liquid. Meanwhile, heat the oil in a small saucepan over medium-low heat. Add the onion and garlic, and cook for three minutes, stirring occasionally. Add the curry powder, coriander, and cinnamon, and cook for two minutes more.

Add the spiced onion mixture, pork, and salt to the soaked bulgur, and mix thoroughly. Form the mixture into 12 neat, oval-shaped cakes about ¾ inch thick and 3 inches long. Place the cakes on a lightly greased baking sheet and cook in the oven for 35 minutes,

turning them over halfway through the cooking time.

In the meantime, make the dressing. In a bowl, mix the yogurt with the mint and lemon juice, and season with some cayenne pepper. Refrigerate the dressing until it is needed.

Warm the pita breads under a broiler for about one minute on each side. Slit each bread along one side and open it to form a pocket. Fill each pocket halfway with some of the shredded lettuce leaves. Spoon a little yogurt dressing into each bread and arrange two hot pork cakes on top. Fill the sides of the pitas with a little more shredded lettuce, and add some slices of cucumber and tomato to each one. Top the filling with a spoonful of the remaining dressing. Serve at once, wrapped in napkins.

Pork Ravioli

Serves 6
Working time: about 1 hour
Total time: about 2 hours

Calories **245**
Protein **18g.**
Cholesterol **80mg.**
Total fat **6g.**
Saturated fat **2g.**
Sodium **240mg.**

¾ lb. pork tenderloin, trimmed of fat and ground or very finely chopped
¼ oz. dried porcini (cepes)
½ oz. sun-dried tomatoes
1 oz. lean prosciutto, finely chopped
¾ cup plain low-fat yogurt
½ tsp. salt
freshly ground black pepper
½ tsp. arrowroot
⅔ cup unsalted vegetable stock (recipe, page 139) or water
1 tbsp. tomato paste
2 fresh tomatoes, peeled, and seeded, for garnish

1 small bunch fresh basil for garnish
Pasta dough
1½ cups unbleached all-purpose flour
¼ cup semolina
1 egg
½ sun-dried tomato, finely chopped (optional)
2 tbsp. tomato paste

To make the ravioli dough, combine the flour, semolina, and egg in a food processor for 30 seconds, or until fine crumbs are formed. Mix the sun-dried tomato, if you are using it, with the tomato paste and 2 tablespoons of hot water. Switch on the processor and pour the tomato and water mixture through the feeder funnel—the pasta dough should form into small lumps, but not one large lump. Switch the processor on again and feed through just enough water to enable the dough to form a single lump. Let the dough rest inside the processor bowl for about 30 minutes.

Soak the dried porcini and dried tomatoes separately in four times their volume of hot water (about ½ cup) for at least 20 minutes. Combine the pork and prosciutto; place them in a heavy-bottomed, nonstick frying pan over medium heat, stirring to break up any lumps that form, until the pork is cooked through—about 10 minutes. Squeeze excess moisture out of the reconstituted porcini and tomatoes. Chop them and add to the meat, retaining the soaking liquids for the pasta sauce. Add one-quarter of the yogurt to the mixture, and season with the salt and some pepper. Let the filling cool a little before making the ravioli.

If using a manual pasta machine, pass the dough at least once through each successive setting on the rollers, flouring lightly whenever the dough feels sticky. You should have four lengths of fairly thin dough, ready to be cut into ravioli. Alternatively, roll out the dough with a rolling pin until it is almost translucent, making two lengths of about the same size.

If you are using a ravioli tray or attachment, follow the manufacturer's instructions; otherwise, simply spoon small piles of the mixture (about 2 teaspoons, or according to the desired size of the ravioli) onto a sheet of rolled-out pasta dough, approximately 1 inch apart. Use a pastry brush to moisten the spaces between with water, then lay a second sheet of pasta dough over the first one. With your fingers, press the pasta between the mounds of filling and along the edges to stick the two sheets together, then cut between the piles of filling with a ravioli cutter, a fluted pastry cutter, or simply a sharp knife.

Bring 2 quarts of water to a boil in a large saucepan and add 1 teaspoon of salt. Add the pasta and cook at a gentle boil until it is fairly tender—10 to 15 minutes, depending on the size of the ravioli.

Meanwhile, prepare the sauce and the garnish. Dissolve the arrowroot in a little of the stock or water, combine it with the remaining stock or water and the two soaking liquids, and bring to a boil, stirring constantly. Simmer until the sauce has thickened slightly, then remove from the heat, and stir in the remaining yogurt and the tomato paste.

Cut the fresh tomatoes into diamond shapes; tear the basil coarsely, leaving the smaller leaves whole. Drain the cooked ravioli thoroughly and season with some pepper. Place the ravioli in a warm serving bowl or in individual dishes, pour the sauce over the ravioli, and garnish with the tomato pieces and basil.

Pork Balls with Capellini

Serves 4
Working (and total) time: about 40 minutes

Calories **280**
Protein **20g.**
Cholesterol **65mg.**
Total fat **12g.**
Saturated fat **6g.**
Sodium **360mg.**

½ lb. pork tenderloin, trimmed of fat and ground or very finely chopped
1 tsp. fennel seeds
2 tbsp. finely chopped parsley
1 tsp. fresh lemon juice
¼ tsp. salt
freshly ground black pepper
1 bay leaf
1 onion
1 carrot
10 black peppercorns
1 cup dry white wine
2 fennel bulbs, feathery tops attached
5 oz. capellini or other thin, long pasta
2 tbsp. unsalted butter
1 tbsp. grated Parmesan cheese

Combine the pork, fennel seeds, parsley, and lemon juice, and season with the salt and some pepper. Set the mixture aside. Put the bay leaf, onion, carrot, pep-percorns, and wine into a heavy-bottomed saucepan, and add water to cover the vegetables. Bring to a boil, then lower the heat to a simmer.

While the stock is simmering, wash the fennel and slice it very thin, cutting out any stringy center or tips; finely chop the feathery tops and reserve for garnishing the dish. With your hands, form the pork mixture into balls about the size of large marbles.

When the stock has simmered for at least 10 minutes, add the fennel to the stock and simmer until it is cooked but still a little crunchy—about five minutes. Strain the stock; reserve the fennel and discard the other solids. Return the stock to the pan, bring to a simmer again, and add the pork. Simmer until the pork is cooked through—about five minutes.

Meanwhile, cook the pasta in 2 quarts of boiling water with 1 teaspoon of salt. Continue cooking until it is *al dente*—about four minutes.

When the pork balls are cooked, add the fennel and cook for a few seconds to warm it through. Drain the pork and fennel, reserving about 4 tablespoons of the cooking liquid. Drain the pasta and return it to the pot with the butter; stir until the butter melts. Stir in the pork and fennel. Divide the mixture among four warmed plates, pour a tablespoon of the reserved liquid over each serving, and scatter the Parmesan and the reserved fennel over the top. Serve immediately.

Saffron Pork with Quail and Shrimp

Serves 4
Working (and total) time: about 1 hour

½ lb. pork tenderloin, trimmed of fat and cut into eight pieces
2 quail
1 tbsp. virgin olive oil
1 red onion, finely chopped
1¼ cups Arborio rice or other round-grain rice
2 pinches saffron threads
½ tsp. salt
freshly ground black pepper
1 quart unsalted chicken stock (recipe, page 139) or water
1 green chili pepper, seeded and finely sliced (caution, page 36)
1 red chili pepper, seeded and finely sliced (caution, page 36)
4 large shrimp, cooked in their shells

Divide each quail in two by cutting down the back and up along the breastbone. Remove any innards that remain, wash the quail pieces, and pat them dry with paper towels. Rub the quail with ½ teaspoon of the olive oil, then set aside.

Heat the remaining olive oil in a heavy paella pan or a frying pan on medium high, and sauté the onion in it for one minute. Add the rice and sauté for about one minute, then add the pork and sauté the whole mixture for another two minutes. Add the saffron, season with the salt and some freshly ground black pepper, and pour on enough chicken stock or water to cover. Bring it slowly to a boil, then simmer the mixture slowly for 35 to 40 minutes, adding stock or water if necessary and stirring occasionally. After 30 minutes, test the rice for doneness. When it is still a little hard but nearly cooked, add the green and red chili peppers and shrimp to heat through.

While the rice mixture is cooking, broil the quail on both sides until they are well browned—approximately 10 minutes.

Transfer the rice and pork mixture to a large dish or individual plates, and serve immediately with the shrimp and quail to one side.

Stuffed Pig's Feet

Serves 8
Working time: about 1 hour and 30 minutes
Total time: about 10 hours (includes chilling)

Calories **220**
Protein **18g.**
Cholesterol **100mg.**
Total fat **16g.**
Saturated fat **3g.**
Sodium **160mg.**

4 pig's feet
2 tsp. salt
2 carrots, sliced
2 onions, peeled and stuck with 3 cloves each
2 ribs celery, sliced
1 bouquet garni (glossary, page 140)
¾ cup dry white wine
⅓ cup wine vinegar
Chicken and pistachio stuffing
¾ lb. finely chopped chicken breast
1 garlic clove, crushed
2 tbsp. finely chopped parsley
2 tbsp. pistachio nuts
2 egg yolks
freshly ground black pepper
Mustard vinaigrette
1 tbsp. wine vinegar
6 tbsp. safflower oil
1 tsp. Dijon mustard
2 tbsp. finely chopped parsley
1 garlic clove, crushed
½ tsp. salt
freshly ground black pepper
2 tbsp. finely cut chives
1 tbsp. chopped capers
1 tbsp. finely chopped gherkin

Rub the pig's feet all over with the salt. Tie each foot firmly between two wooden skewers (*Step 1, below*), and put them into a large pan with the carrots, onions, celery, bouquet garni, white wine, and wine vinegar. Cover the ingredients with water and bring to a boil; cover tightly and simmer for five and a half hours.

Take the pan off the heat. Remove the feet and set them aside. Strain the liquid, discard the solids, and return the stock to the pan. Set the feet aside until they are cool enough to handle. Meanwhile, mix together the chicken, garlic, parsley, pistachio nuts, egg yolks, and some pepper until they are well blended.

Cut the strings around the feet and take out all the bones (*Step 2, below*). Sandwich the stuffing between the feet as described in Step 3; wrap the package in muslin or cheesecloth, then simmer the feet for another hour in the stock.

Take the stuffed feet out of the liquid to cool. Chill in the refrigerator for at least two and a half hours, or preferably overnight. To prepare the vinaigrette, put the wine vinegar, oil, mustard, parsley, garlic, salt, and some pepper into a jar, and shake well, then stir in the chives, capers, and gherkin. When the feet are thoroughly chilled, unwrap them and slice thinly, and serve accompanied by the vinaigrette.

SUGGESTED ACCOMPANIMENT: *watercress and orange salad.*

Preparing Stuffed Pig's Feet

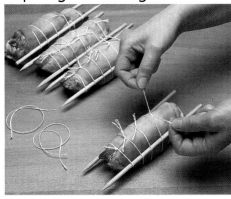

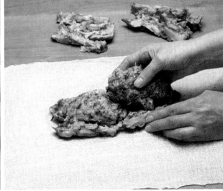

1 BRACING THE PIG'S FEET. To ensure that the feet do not disintegrate while cooking, brace each one with two strong wooden skewers about 2 inches longer than the foot. Secure the skewers with string tied around the foot at intervals of about 1 inch.

2 REMOVING THE BONES. After poaching the feet in stock, cut away the string and discard the skewers. Split open each foot lengthwise by cutting from the hooves to the opposite end, then carefully pick out all the pieces of bone.

3 STUFFING THE FEET. Lay two split feet end to end in the middle of a piece of muslin or cheesecloth about 20 by 16 inches. Spread a layer of prepared stuffing over the feet, then place two more pig's feet split side down on top of the stuffing.

Roast Pork Salad with Mustard Vinaigrette

Serves 4
Working (and total) time: about 10 minutes

Calories **245**	¾ lb. cold roast pork
Protein **26g.**	¼ lb. lettuce leaves, washed and dried
Cholesterol **60mg.**	2 tsp. sherry vinegar or red wine vinegar
Total fat **14g.**	2 tsp. fresh lemon juice
Saturated fat **4g.**	2 tsp. Dijon mustard
Sodium **270mg.**	1 tbsp. virgin olive oil
	1 tbsp. safflower oil
	¼ cup cut chives
	½ tsp. salt
	freshly ground black pepper

Divide the lettuce leaves among four individual plates. Slice the pork as thin as possible and arrange it over the lettuce. Whisk the vinegar, lemon juice, and mustard together in a bowl, then add the olive and safflower oils and whisk again until thoroughly mixed. Add the chives, and season with the salt and some freshly ground black pepper, then pour the mustard vinaigrette over the pork and lettuce.

SUGGESTED ACCOMPANIMENT: *crusty bread.*

Phyllo Parcels

Serves 4
Working time: about 45 minutes
Total time: about 4 hours (includes marinating)

Calories **280**
Protein **23g.**
Cholesterol **70mg.**
Total fat **15g.**
Saturated fat **4g.**
Sodium **100mg.**

1 lb. lean pork, trimmed of fat and cut into ¾-inch cubes
½ cup red wine
2 garlic cloves, crushed
1 tsp. fresh thyme, bruised
1 tsp. mixed peppercorns, coarsely crushed
½ oz. dried porcini (cepes)
½ tsp. salt
4 large spinach leaves, stems removed, or about 8 smaller leaves
2 sheets phyllo pastry
2 tbsp. safflower oil
4 tsp. red-currant jelly

Put the wine, garlic, thyme, and peppercorns into a nonreactive dish, and add the meat. Cover the dish and set it aside to marinate in a cool place for at least three hours. Meanwhile, soak the porcini in hot water for 20 minutes.

Drain the meat and pat the cubes dry on paper towels. Reserve any marinade that has not been absorbed. Remove the porcini from the soaking liquid, then rinse, dry, and chop them coarsely.

Sauté the meat in a dry, nonstick frying pan over medium-high heat, turning the pieces regularly, until the cubes are well browned on all sides and cooked through—about 20 minutes. Stir in the chopped mushrooms, the reserved marinade, and the salt. Cook until all of the liquid is evaporated, then remove the pan from the heat.

Plunge the spinach leaves into rapidly boiling water, drain immediately, refresh under cold running water, and lay the leaves out in a single layer on several thicknesses of paper towels.

Preheat the oven to 375° F.

Cut each phyllo sheet in half lengthwise to make four long, broad strips. Position one strip with a short side toward you and brush it lightly with some of the oil. Place one large spinach leaf—or two or three smaller, overlapping leaves—at the end of the strip, then one-quarter of the meat mixture in a pile on the spinach. Lift one corner of the strip and fold it over so that the corner meets the opposite long side, then fold the package toward the far end of the strip. Continue folding alternately across and up the strip until you reach the far end; any short band of phyllo remaining at the far end may be trimmed off or folded around the package. Repeat with the other strips and the rest of the spinach and meat.

Brush the packages lightly with the remaining oil and place them on a nonstick baking sheet. Bake in the oven for 20 minutes, turning them over once, until they are golden and crisp.

Serve the phyllo parcels hot, with a spoonful of red-currant jelly on the side.

SUGGESTED ACCOMPANIMENTS: *steamed broccoli; red-leaf lettuce salad.*

Manicotti Stuffed with Pork and Ricotta

Serves 4
Working (and total) time: about 1 hour

Calories **460**
Protein **28g.**
Cholesterol **45mg.**
Total fat **20g.**
Saturated fat **6g.**
Sodium **145mg.**

½ lb. pork tenderloin, trimmed of fat and ground or chopped
2 oz. sun-dried tomatoes
½ cup low-fat ricotta
1 oz. fresh basil, finely chopped
freshly ground black pepper
8 manicotti tubes
4 cups unsalted vegetable or chicken stock (recipes, page 139)
Pesto sauce
1½ cups packed fresh basil leaves
1 oz. pine nuts
3 tbsp. virgin olive oil
1 garlic clove
1 oz. freshly grated Parmesan cheese

Cut one of the sun-dried tomatoes into strips and reserve for a garnish. Chop the remaining tomatoes finely, and mix them well with the pork, ricotta, basil, and some black pepper. Using your fingers, fill the dry manicotti with this stuffing mixture. To make the pesto sauce, put the basil, pine nuts, oil, and garlic into a food processor or a blender, and blend for two minutes. Add the Parmesan and blend again briefly.

Bring the stock to a simmer in a pan large enough to hold the manicotti in one layer. Using a slotted spoon, carefully put the filled manicotti into the stock and poach until the pasta is soft and the stuffing feels firm—about 15 minutes. Drain off and reserve the stock, and keep the manicotti warm.

Blend 4 tablespoons of the warm stock with 2 tablespoons of the pesto sauce. Reheat the sauce slightly if necessary. Keep any remaining pesto for another use. Arrange the manicotti on a warmed serving dish, pour a thick ribbon of sauce over them, and garnish with the reserved sun-dried tomato strips.

Meatballs with Greens

Serves 4
Working time: about 25 minutes
Total time: about 40 minutes (includes marinating)

Calories **170**
Protein **22g.**
Cholesterol **70mg.**
Total fat **8g.**
Saturated fat **3g.**
Sodium **490mg.**

1 lb. lean pork, trimmed of fat and cut into 2-inch chunks
1 oz. arugula or watercress leaves (about ½ cup)
½ tsp. ground allspice
½ tsp. salt
freshly ground black pepper
4 tbsp. plain low-fat yogurt
2 tsp. balsamic vinegar, or 1½ tsp. red wine vinegar, plus ½ tsp. honey

Yogurt dip

4 tbsp. plain low-fat yogurt
2 tsp. balsamic vinegar, or 1½ tsp. red wine vinegar, plus ½ tsp. honey

1 tsp. coriander seeds, roasted and crushed
¼ tsp. salt

In a food processor, finely chop the pork with the arugula, allspice, salt, and some pepper. Form the mixture into 16 balls. Blend the yogurt and vinegar in a bowl, and roll the balls in this mixture; set them aside to marinate for 15 minutes, turning them occasionally.

Preheat the broiler. Place the meatballs and marinade on a broiling pan, and broil about 10 minutes, turning and basting from time to time, until the meatballs are golden brown and cooked through.

To make the dip, mix the cooking juices from the meatballs with the yogurt, balsamic vinegar, coriander, and salt. Serve the meatballs hot with the dip in a bowl alongside them.

SUGGESTED ACCOMPANIMENT: *green salad including arugula or watercress.*

Pork with Nappa Cabbage in Steamed Buns

Serves 6
Working time: about 50 minutes
Total time: about 2 hours and 20 minutes

Calories **340**
Protein **19g.**
Cholesterol **30mg.**
Total fat **14g.**
Saturated fat **3g.**
Sodium **450mg.**

¾ lb. cooked roast pork loin, trimmed of fat and diced
1 cake (.6 oz.) fresh yeast, or 1 envelope (¼ oz.) active dry yeast, plus 1 tsp. sugar
2 cups all-purpose flour
1 tsp. baking powder
1 tbsp. solid vegetable shortening
1 tbsp. sesame oil
½ lb. Nappa cabbage leaves, finely shredded
1 tsp. salt
1 tbsp. safflower oil
1 tsp. finely grated fresh ginger
2 garlic cloves, finely chopped
¾ cup finely chopped scallions
1 tbsp. rice wine or dry sherry
1 tbsp. low-sodium soy sauce
2 tbsp. hoisin or barbecue sauce

Dissolve the fresh yeast in ½ cup of warm water; if using dry yeast, mix the sugar and yeast together with ½ cup of warm water, and set the mixture aside for 10 minutes, until it is foamy. Sift the flour and baking powder together into a large bowl, and cut in the shortening. Mix the frothy yeast liquid into the flour and shortening, and knead well. Cover the dough loosely with plastic wrap and set aside until doubled in volume—about one hour.

Flatten the dough, then divide it into 12 balls. Roll the balls into circles about 4 inches in diameter. Brush the circles lightly with a little of the sesame oil, then fold them over into semicircles and place each on a square of lightly oiled wax paper. Cover loosely with plastic wrap and let them rise again for 30 minutes. Steam the semicircles in a single layer, partially covered, over boiling water for 20 minutes.

Meanwhile, sprinkle the shredded Nappa cabbage with the salt and set it aside for 20 minutes. Rinse the leaves well under cold running water, then squeeze them dry with your hands.

Heat the safflower oil in a frying pan over medium-high heat, and fry the ginger, garlic, and scallions for a minute or two, stirring all the time. Add the rice wine or sherry, soy sauce, hoisin or barbecue sauce, and the remaining sesame oil, then reduce the sauce until it is very thick and syrupy. Stir in the cabbage leaves and the diced pork.

Serve the buns straight from the steamer with the hot pork mixture. Each diner takes a bun, splits it, and spoons in some of the filling.

EDITOR'S NOTE: *A bamboo steamer provides a wider, flatter surface than an ordinary steamer. The bamboo steamer may be placed over a wok containing boiling water.*

Italian Meat Loaf with Tomato Sauce

Serves 6
Working time: about 25 minutes
Total time: about 1 hour and 10 minutes

Calories **250**
Protein **28g.**
Cholesterol **80mg.**
Total fat **11g.**
Saturated fat **4g.**
Sodium **130mg.**

1½ lb. pork tenderloin, ground or very finely chopped
1 garlic clove, finely chopped
¼ cup fresh bread crumbs
1 tbsp. tomato paste
2 tbsp. dry white wine
1 oz. sun-dried tomatoes, finely chopped
1 oz. fresh basil, finely chopped (about ¼ cup)
freshly ground black pepper

Tomato sauce

1 tbsp. virgin olive oil
1 large onion, finely chopped
2 garlic cloves, finely chopped
2 lb. tomatoes, peeled and chopped, or 28 oz. canned whole tomatoes
1 fresh bay leaf
2 tsp. finely chopped sun-dried tomatoes
freshly ground black pepper
1½ oz. dried porcini (cepes), soaked for 20 minutes in hot water, or ½ lb. chopped fresh mushrooms, sautéed until soft in 1 tbsp. butter
1 oz. fresh basil, torn into small pieces (about ⅓ cup)

Preheat the oven to 350° F. Combine the pork, garlic, bread crumbs, tomato paste, wine, tomatoes, basil, and some pepper, and mix them together well. Line a 1-pound loaf pan with wax paper and press the meat-loaf mixture into it. Bake in the oven for one hour.

While the meat loaf is cooking, prepare the sauce. Heat the olive oil in a heavy-bottomed frying pan over medium heat, and cook the onion and garlic until they are translucent—about five minutes. Add the tomatoes, bay leaf, and the sun-dried tomatoes; season with some black pepper and cook for 20 minutes. Drain the porcini, if using, and chop them into pieces of roughly equal size. When the sauce is cooked, remove the bay leaf from the pan, and add the porcini or mushrooms and the basil. Reheat the sauce to warm the porcini.

Serve the meat loaf cut into thick slices with the sauce spooned around it.

SUGGESTED ACCOMPANIMENT: *crusty bread.*

4 *Tender pork chops cooked in the microwave oven with fennel are finished with an orange and Madeira glaze (recipe, opposite).*

Pork in the Microwave Oven

The advantages of the microwave oven in terms of convenience for the cook are well known—it cooks food far more rapidly than a conventional oven, it is easy to clean and cheap to run, and it takes up very little space in the kitchen. The recipes in this chapter have been chosen to demonstrate that there are benefits for the diner also, and that the appearance and flavor of certain dishes are actually improved by cooking in the microwave oven.

Because the process of mincing or grinding breaks down the meat's fibers, ground pork is particularly suited to rapid cooking in the microwave oven. Chops also benefit from microwave cooking. When chops are fried, grilled, or broiled, the time required for the meat around the bone to cook through properly can cause the outside of the chops to become dried out and tough; in the microwave oven, the chops will cook through evenly, so that the inside will be ready at the same time as the outside.

The speed of microwave cooking is most evident in the case of stews and casserole dishes. The recipe for pork in cider on page 131, for example, requires only 15 minutes in the oven plus another five minutes for thickening the liquid, and all the other casserole recipes in this chapter can be cooked in well under an hour. A microwave oven also provides the quickest means of preparing the constituent ingredients—such as the winter squash in the golden casserole on page 133—and of reheating a casserole cooked in advance.

Several of the recipes in this chapter call for the use of a browning dish, a ceramic-glass broiling pan or dish with a tin-oxide coating that colors the meat in the same way as the initial searing at high temperatures in conventional cooking. Always follow the manufacturer's instructions strictly when using this dish, as overheating can damage it. Also, when covering a microwave dish containing liquid with wax paper or microwave-safe plastic wrap, take care to leave one corner loose to prevent a buildup of steam.

The recipes have been tested in 650-watt and 700-watt ovens. Power settings often vary among different microwave ovens, but in the recipes that follow, "high" indicates 100 percent power, "medium high" 70 percent, "medium" 50 percent, and "medium low" 30 percent power. Because food continues to cook for a short while after it is removed from the oven, it is important to guard against overcooking by using the shortest time specified. You can then test for doneness after letting the dish stand for a minute or so, and return it to the oven if necessary.

Florence Fennel Chops

Serves 4
Working (and total) time: about 20 minutes

Calories **200**
Protein **25g.**
Cholesterol **80mg.**
Total fat **8g.**
Saturated fat **3g.**
Sodium **420mg.**

4 boned pork loin chops (about 4 oz. each), trimmed of fat
2 fennel bulbs (about ¼ lb. each)
3 tbsp. fresh orange juice
1 tbsp. Madeira
½ tsp. arrowroot
⅔ cup unsalted vegetable stock (recipe, page 139)
1 tsp. salt
ground white pepper
½ tsp. ground fennel seeds (optional)
Orange glaze
1 tbsp. fresh orange juice, plus 1 tsp. grated orange zest
1 tbsp. honey
1 tbsp. Madeira
1 tbsp. balsamic vinegar, or 1 tbsp. red wine vinegar, plus 1 tsp. honey

Divide each fennel bulb into eight sections. Place the fennel in a dish with the orange juice and Madeira, and microwave on high until the fennel is just tender—seven to eight minutes. Preheat a 2-quart browning dish on high for five to seven minutes, or for the maximum time allowed in the manufacturer's instructions. Dry the chops and arrange them in the dish with the thickest part to the outside, pressing them down hard onto the browning surface with a spatula. Once the sizzling stops, cook the chops on high for one minute; then turn them to brown the other side.

Mix the arrowroot with the stock and stir into the fennel. Pour the mixture around the chops, and cook on high until the liquid begins to bubble and thicken —about one minute. Stir well, lower the setting to medium, and cook, covered, until tender—two to three minutes. Stir and give the dish a quarter turn every minute. Remove the dish from the oven and let it rest for two minutes. Test for doneness by cutting through the thickest part of a chop with the point of a knife; if the meat appears pink, cook for one minute more on medium and test. Repeat as necessary, taking care not to overcook. When the pork is done, allow the chops to rest for two to three minutes.

Combine the orange juice and zest, honey, Madeira, and balsamic vinegar in a small dish. Cook on high until the glaze is syrupy—two and a half to three minutes. Brush some of the glaze carefully over the chops in their dish. Add the remaining glaze to the fennel sauce and cook on high for 30 to 60 seconds, stirring halfway through. Add the salt, some white pepper, and the fennel seeds, if you wish. Serve immediately.

Stuffed Pork Chops with Kidney Bean and Juniper Sauce

Serves 4
Working time: about 20 minutes
Total time: about 35 minutes

Calories **425**	
Protein **40g.**	4 pork chops (4½ to 5 oz. each), trimmed of fat
Cholesterol **70mg.**	3 tbsp. pine nuts
Total fat **15g.**	3 tbsp. cooked long-grain white rice
Saturated fat **5g.**	4 fresh or dried dates, pitted
Sodium **110mg.**	1½ tsp. fresh rosemary, or ½ tsp. dried rosemary
	1 tbsp. safflower oil

Kidney bean and juniper sauce

1½ cups cooked drained kidney beans
freshly ground black pepper
18 juniper berries
1 cup unsalted vegetable stock (recipe, page 139)
2 tbsp. tomato paste

In a food processor, blend together the pine nuts, the long-grain white rice, the dates, and the rosemary. (Alternatively, chop the rice, dates, and pine nuts, and mix them by hand with the rosemary.) Cut a pocket in the side of each of the pork chops and press the stuffing mixture into the pockets *(technique, page 12)*.

Preheat a browning dish for five to seven minutes, or for the maximum time allowed in the manufacturer's instructions, and swirl the safflower oil around the bottom of the dish. Pat the pork chops dry with paper towels to facilitate browning, and arrange them in the dish with the thickest part to the outside, pressing them down onto the browning surface with a spatula. When the sizzling stops, cook the chops on high for one minute before turning them over to brown the other side.

To make the sauce, puree the kidney beans, some black pepper, the juniper berries, stock, and tomato paste together in a food processor or a blender, and pour the mixture into a shallow dish. Arrange the chops over the puree with the thicker part toward the outside of the dish.

Microwave on high, uncovered, until the chops are just cooked—about seven minutes. Remove the chops from the dish and keep them warm.

Return the dish to the microwave, and cook the sauce on high for three minutes to reduce and thicken it, stirring once during cooking. Pour the sauce onto the chops and serve immediately.

SUGGESTED ACCOMPANIMENTS: *broccoli florets; microwaved tomato halves.*

Celery Chops

Serves 4
Working time: about 15 minutes
Total time: about 40 minutes

Calories **200**
Protein **25g.**
Cholesterol **70mg.**
Total fat **9g.**
Saturated fat **4g.**
Sodium **390mg.**

4 boned pork loin chops (about 4 oz. each), trimmed of fat
¾ lb. celery, cut into 1-inch pieces (about 2 cups)
⅔ cup stout
⅔ cup unsalted vegetable stock (recipe, page 139)
½ onion, sliced
1 tsp. arrowroot, dissolved in 1 tbsp. stout, stock, or water
1 to 2 tbsp. prepared English grainy mustard
⅓ cup plain low-fat yogurt
2 tbsp. torn celery leaves
½ tsp. salt
freshly ground black pepper

Place the celery in a dish with the stout, stock, and onion, and cover the dish with plastic wrap, leaving one corner open. Bring to a boil on high, then cook on high, stirring several times, until the celery is tender—approximately 15 minutes.

Preheat a browning dish on high for five to seven minutes, or for the maximum time allowed in the manufacturer's instructions. Quickly arrange the chops in the dish with the thickest part to the outside and press down hard onto the browning surface with the aid of a spatula. Once the sizzling stops, cook the chops on high for one minute, then turn them over to brown the other side lightly.

Pour the vegetables and their cooking liquid around the chops, and cook on high for another minute, or until the liquid bubbles. Lower the setting to medium and cook for three minutes, covered, giving the dish a quarter turn every minute. Allow to rest for two minutes, then test for doneness by cutting through the thickest part of a chop with the point of a sharp knife. If the meat is no longer pink, the chops are cooked through; if the meat appears pink, cook for just one minute more and test as before. Repeat the process as necessary, but take care not to overcook the chops. When the meat is fully cooked, remove the pork and vegetables, leaving the cooking liquid in the dish, and keep them warm while you make the sauce.

Stir the arrowroot mixture and 1 tablespoon of the mustard into the cooking liquid. Cook the sauce on high for one to two minutes, until thickened, stirring every 20 seconds or so. Whisk the yogurt into the cooking liquid. Add the celery leaves, the salt, some pepper, and the remaining mustard to taste. Pour the sauce over the pork and celery, and serve immediately.

Winter Fruited Chops

Serves 4
Working (and total) time: about 30 minutes

Calories **180**
Protein **25g.**
Cholesterol **70mg.**
Total fat **8g.**
Saturated fat **3g.**
Sodium **260mg.**

4 pork loin chops (4½ to 5 oz. each), trimmed of fat
2 tbsp. grainy mustard
12 fresh sage leaves
½ tsp. salt
2 slices orange, halved
2 tsp. dry mustard (optional)
4 tbsp. cranberry sauce or red-currant jelly
2 cups fresh cranberries, chopped
2 tbsp. port
freshly ground black pepper

With a sharp knife, cut a pocket in the boneless side of each chop *(technique, page 12)*. Spread ½ tablespoon of the mustard over the surfaces of each pocket and press three sage leaves onto the mustard. Sprinkle with a little of the salt and place a half slice of orange in each pocket.

Dust one side of each chop with ½ teaspoon of the dry mustard, if you are using it. Spread 1 tablespoon of the cranberry sauce or red-currant jelly over the powdered side of each chop, and press the fresh berries firmly into the sauce.

Arrange the chops in a dish with the thickest part toward the outside of the dish. Microwave on medium for four minutes, turning the dish once during this time, then rearrange the chops with a spatula to ensure that they will be evenly cooked. Cook for six to eight minutes more on medium, giving the dish a quarter turn at least three times during this period. Remove from the oven.

Allow the chops to rest in the dish for two minutes, then test for doneness by cutting into the thickest part of the meat near the bone with the point of a sharp knife; if no pink meat is visible (allowing for pink staining by the fruit juice), the chops are cooked through. If the meat still appears pink, cook for one to two minutes more on medium, then test as before. Remove the chops from the dish and keep them warm.

To make a quick, light sauce, reduce the cooking juices in the dish by microwaving on high for two to three minutes; add the port and reduce the sauce further on high until it is slightly syrupy. Season with the remaining salt and some black pepper, and spoon the sauce over the chops.

EDITOR'S NOTE: *If a slightly sweeter flavor is preferred to balance the sourness of the cranberries, spread a little red-currant jelly or light brown sugar over the orange slices and the cranberries.*

Chops with Eggplant Puree and Vegetables

Serves 4
Working (and total) time: about 45 minutes

Calories **250**
Protein **26g.**
Cholesterol **70mg.**
Total fat **13g.**
Saturated fat **3g.**
Sodium **370mg.**

4 pork loin chops, boned (about 4 oz. each), trimmed of fat	
1 lb. eggplant	
1 tsp. virgin olive oil	
½ cup plain low-fat yogurt	
1 tsp. salt	
½ tsp. ground coriander	
¼ tsp. ground cumin	
4 small sprigs fresh mint (optional)	
freshly ground black pepper	
Mediterranean vegetables	
2 zucchini, sliced	
1 sweet red pepper, seeded, deribbed, and sliced	
1 sweet yellow or green pepper, seeded, deribbed, and sliced	
1 tomato, sliced	
1 tbsp. virgin olive oil	
½ garlic clove, finely chopped	
1 tbsp. finely chopped cilantro	

Pierce the skin of the eggplant in several places with the point of a knife. Brush the skin with about ½ teaspoon of the oil, place the eggplant on a double thickness of paper towels, and cook on high for five minutes, turning the eggplant twice during this time. The eggplant should be soft, but not collapsed, and the skin fairly tender. When the eggplant is cool enough to handle, slice it into ¾-inch-thick rounds.

Preheat a browning dish on high for five to seven minutes, or for the maximum time allowed in the manufacturer's instructions. Dry the chops with paper towels and brush them with the remaining oil. When the browning dish is ready, quickly arrange the chops in it with the thickest part to the outside of the dish; press down hard with the aid of a spatula. Once the sizzling stops, cook the chops on high for one minute, then turn them over to lightly brown the other side.

Remove the chops and arrange the eggplant slices in the dish. Place the chops on top of the eggplant. Cover the dish with a lid or with wax paper, and cook on medium for five minutes, giving the dish a quarter turn every minute. Allow the chops to rest for two minutes, then test for doneness by cutting through the thickest part of a chop with the point of a knife; if no pink meat is visible, the chops are cooked through. If the meat is still pink, cook for one minute more on medium and test as before. Repeat as necessary, but take care not to overcook the chops. When fully cooked, remove the chops and keep them warm.

To prepare the vegetables, mix together the zucchini, sweet red and yellow or green peppers, and tomato with the oil, garlic, and cilantro. Microwave on high for three minutes. To make the puree, blend or process together the eggplant, yogurt, salt, coriander, cumin, and mint, if you are using it. The puree should still be quite thick; if you wish, add any cooking juices that the eggplant did not absorb. Add some pepper, and serve warm with the chops and vegetables.

EDITOR'S NOTE: *When seasoning the puree, you may wish to sweeten it by stirring in 1 teaspoon of honey.*

Pork and Barley Hot Pot

Serves 8
Working time: about 35 minutes
Total time: about 9 hours (includes soaking)

Calories **165**
Protein **13g.**
Cholesterol **45mg.**
Total fat **6g.**
Saturated fat **2g.**
Sodium **75mg.**

1 lb. pork tenderloin, trimmed and cut into 1-inch cubes
½ cup pearl barley
2½ cups unsalted chicken stock (recipe, page 139)
1 tbsp. safflower oil
½ lb. pearl onions, peeled
1 tbsp. dark brown sugar
½ lb. carrots, cut into small sticks
1 tbsp. chopped fresh rosemary, or 1 tsp. dried rosemary
freshly ground black pepper
4 oz. green beans, trimmed
1 tbsp. cornstarch
1 cup shelled peas, or frozen peas, thawed

Put the barley and stock into a covered bowl, and refrigerate overnight to soften and swell the barley.

The next day, put the oil into a large casserole with the onions and sugar, stir well, and microwave on high until the onions brown slightly—about five minutes. Add the pork and microwave on high for three minutes, stirring once. Stir in the undrained barley, carrots, rosemary, and some pepper. Cover the dish and microwave on high for about 11 minutes; stir occasionally. Add the beans to the casserole and cook until the meat and vegetables are almost tender—approximately four minutes more.

Blend the cornstarch with 2 tablespoons of cold water and stir the mixture into the hot pot. Microwave on high, uncovered, until the liquid boils—about three minutes. Remove the dish from the oven, add the peas, and stir; set the dish aside for one to two minutes to allow the peas to cook through, then serve.

Cider Pork

Serves 6
Working time: about 25 minutes
Total time: about 5 hours (includes marinating)

Calories **195**
Protein **17g.**
Cholesterol **70mg.**
Total fat **10g.**
Saturated fat **4g.**
Sodium **80mg.**

1½ lb. pork tenderloin, trimmed and cut into 1-inch cubes
1 garlic clove, crushed
1 tbsp. walnut oil
⅔ cup cider or apple juice
1 orange, grated zest and juice
2 tsp. fresh lemon juice
1 tbsp. fresh thyme, or 1 tsp. dried thyme leaves
½ tsp. grated fresh ginger
freshly ground black pepper
4 tsp. arrowroot, dissolved in 3 tbsp. cider

In a large casserole, mix together the garlic, walnut oil, cider or apple juice, orange zest and juice, lemon juice, thyme, ginger, and some pepper. Stir in the pork, cover, and let it marinate in the refrigerator for four to six hours. Stir the meat once or twice during this time to make sure the cubes are evenly marinated.

Place the covered casserole in the oven and microwave on medium until the meat is tender—about 10 minutes. Stir once during cooking. Pour the arrowroot mixture into the casserole and microwave on high, stirring once during cooking, until the liquid thickens—about five minutes. Serve hot.

SUGGESTED ACCOMPANIMENT: *saffron rice.*

Greek Casserole

Serves 4
Working time: about 15 minutes
Total time: about 1 hour

Calories **290**
Protein **23g.**
Cholesterol **70mg.**
Total fat **8g.**
Saturated fat **3g.**
Sodium **400mg.**

1 lb. lean boneless roasting pork, cut into 1-inch cubes
1 tbsp. flour, seasoned with ground white pepper
1 tsp. virgin olive oil
1½ cups unsalted veal or vegetable stock (recipes, page 139)
¾ lb. small new potatoes, or larger potatoes cut into 1-inch chunks
4 dried pear halves
2 tbsp. chunky quince preserves or orange marmalade
2 tbsp. honey
4 sprigs fresh thyme
½ cinnamon stick
2 strips lemon zest (about 2 inches each)
¾ cup retsina or dry vermouth
1 tsp. salt
4 to 6 tbsp. fresh lemon juice
freshly ground black pepper

Preheat a 2-quart browning dish on high for five to seven minutes, or for the maximum time allowed in the manufacturer's instructions. Toss the meat in the seasoned flour. Brush the dish with the oil and add the meat. Cook on high for two minutes, turning the pieces several times so that the meat browns evenly.

Heat the stock until it is almost boiling. Add ¼ cup of the stock to the meat and cook for two minutes more on high, scraping the dish with a spatula to detach the browned bits and thicken the sauce. Add the potatoes, pears, quince preserves or marmalade, honey, thyme, cinnamon, lemon zest, and retsina or vermouth, and enough stock to cover the meat (which may otherwise discolor slightly). Continue to cook on high until the liquid comes to a boil—10 to 15 minutes. Stir the contents of the dish; cover and cook for another 30 to 45 minutes on medium low, until the meat is tender. Stir the contents of the dish once or twice during this time, and add more stock if the liquid in the dish falls below the level of the meat.

Toward the end of the cooking time, add the salt and enough lemon juice to cut the sweetness pleasantly; a little more honey may be added if a sweeter taste is desired. Remove the cinnamon stick and thyme sprigs, season with some pepper, and serve hot.

SUGGESTED ACCOMPANIMENT: *crusty bread.*

Golden Casserole

THIS NOURISHING DISH MAKES A COMPLETE MEAL AND NEEDS
NO ACCOMPANIMENT.

Serves 4
Working time: about 30 minutes
Total time: about 1 hour and 30 minutes

Calories **270**
Protein **24g.**
Cholesterol **70mg.**
Total fat **8g.**
Saturated fat **3g.**
Sodium **300mg.**

1 lb. pork tenderloin, trimmed of fat and cut into 1-inch cubes
1 tbsp. safflower oil
¾ lb. acorn, butternut, or other winter squash
2 sweet potatoes (about ¾ lb.)
¼ tsp. saffron threads
½ tsp. salt
1½ cups unsalted vegetable stock (recipe, page 139)
⅛ tsp. ground mace
2 whole allspice berries
½ lb. yellow summer squash or other summer squash
4 oz. frozen baby corn

Preheat a browning dish for five to seven minutes, or for the maximum time allowed in the manufacturer's instructions. Add the oil and the pork, and stir vigorously until the meat is lightly browned—about one and a half minutes. Transfer the meat to a casserole.

Pierce the skin of the winter squash in two or three places with a skewer or a sharp knife, then microwave it on high, on a double thickness of paper towels, for five minutes—it will now be soft and easy to cut. Peel and cut into 1-inch cubes. Peel the sweet potatoes, cut them into 1-inch cubes, and place them in the casserole with the meat. Using a mortar and pestle, grind the saffron with ¼ teaspoon of the salt until it is pulverized. Warm the stock, dissolve the saffron and salt in it, and pour the liquid into the casserole. Add the mace and allspice, and microwave on high until the liquid begins to boil—approximately five minutes. Stir the contents of the casserole and cook for another 15 minutes on medium low.

Remove the casserole from the microwave and add the winter squash. Cook the casserole for another 10 minutes on medium low.

Cut the summer squash into pieces slightly smaller than the rest of the vegetables and the meat. Wash the corn. Add the summer squash and corn to the casserole, and cook for a final 10 minutes on medium low.

Remove the allspice and add the remaining salt. The golden liquid will be clear and thin. Serve hot.

EDITOR'S NOTE: *In place of the tenderloin, you can substitute a more dense, muscular cut such as leg or shoulder in this recipe. Trim the meat of all visible fat, and allow about 15 minutes longer cooking time before adding the summer squash and corn [for the final 10 minutes of cooking].*

Kofta with Curry Sauce and Cucumber

COMMON IN INDIAN AND MIDDLE EASTERN COOKING, KOFTA
CONSISTS OF GROUND MEAT WITH SEASONINGS SHAPED
INTO BALLS OR CYLINDERS.

Serves 8
Working (and total) time: about 55 minutes

Calories **230**
Protein **22g.**
Cholesterol **65mg.**
Total fat **11g.**
Saturated fat **3g.**
Sodium **275mg.**

1½ lb. lean ground pork
¼ tsp. chili powder
1½ tsp. ground turmeric
1 tsp. ground cardamom
½ tsp. salt
½-inch piece fresh ginger, chopped
2 tbsp. besan flour or soy flour
2 tsp. finely chopped cilantro
1 tsp. finely chopped parsley
1 cucumber, sliced into 1½-inch lengths and quartered

Curry sauce

2 tbsp. safflower oil
1 large onion, very finely chopped
1 garlic clove, crushed
1-inch piece cinnamon stick
4 cloves
2 tbsp. ground coriander
2 tbsp. ground cumin
¼ tsp. chili powder
1 bay leaf
½ tsp. salt
½ lb. potatoes, grated
1 lb. ripe tomatoes, peeled and seeded, or 14 oz. canned whole tomatoes

To prepare the sauce, first preheat a large, deep browning dish for five to seven minutes, or for the maximum time allowed in the manufacturer's instructions. Add the oil and onion, and microwave, uncovered, on high, stirring occasionally, until the onion is soft and slightly brown—about five minutes. Stir in the garlic, cinnamon stick, cloves, coriander, cumin, chili powder, bay leaf, and salt, and microwave on high for 30 seconds. Add the potatoes, tomatoes, and 2 cups of water; cover and cook on high for 20 minutes, stirring occasionally.

While the sauce is cooking, put the chili powder, turmeric, cardamom, salt, ginger, and flour into a bowl, add the chopped cilantro and parsley, and mix together. Shape the mixture into 16 sausage shapes or balls, and set them aside.

When the sauce has finished cooking, remove the cinnamon stick and the bay leaf and discard them. Puree the sauce in a food processor or a blender, pass it through a sieve, then return the sauce to the browning dish. Arrange the kofta in the dish, cover, and microwave on high for five minutes. Rearrange the kofta, exchanging those in the center with the ones around the edges. Baste the kofta with the curry sauce and microwave on high for two minutes, then add the cucumber pieces and cook for one minute more.

SUGGESTED ACCOMPANIMENTS: *popadams; boiled rice.*

EDITOR'S NOTE: *Popadams may be microwaved on high until they are puffy—about one minute. Besan flour is made from dried chick-peas; it is available in Indian markets.*

Herbed Scrolls with Leek

Serves 4
Working (and total) time: about 40 minutes

Calories **250**
Protein **21g.**
Cholesterol **70mg.**
Total fat **12g.**
Saturated fat **3g.**
Sodium **110mg.**

1 lb. pork tenderloin, trimmed of fat
1 large leek
1 egg white
½ tsp. salt
¼ cup low-fat ricotta cheese
2 tbsp. plain low-fat yogurt
3 tbsp. finely chopped mixed fresh herbs
1 tbsp. herbed oil or virgin olive oil
Honey glaze
4 tbsp. honey
1 tbsp. fresh lime or lemon juice
1 tbsp. fresh orange juice
1 tbsp. balsamic vinegar, or 1 tbsp. red wine vinegar, plus 1 tsp. honey
1 tbsp. low-sodium soy sauce
2 sprigs fresh thyme, or ½ tsp. dried thyme leaves
1 tsp. arrowroot, dissolved in 1 tsp. orange juice or water

Cut the pork diagonally into 20 thin rounds, then pound them with a mallet until they are three times larger *(technique, page 12)*. Set the rounds aside.

Cut off three or four of the leek's outer leaves and wash them. Blanch the leaves for two minutes on high in lightly salted, boiling water, then rinse the leaves in cold water and spread them out on paper towels to dry. Finely slice the white part of the leek, blanch it for two to three minutes, and drain it.

Whisk the egg white with the salt until it is fairly stiff. Beat together the ricotta and yogurt, mixed herbs, and the white slices of leek, then fold in the egg white. Divide this mixture among the pieces of pork, leaving a narrow border around the edges, then roll up the pieces and put them on a plate, seam side down. Cut the outer leek leaves into 20 thin strips and tie the stuffed scrolls with these ribbons, with the knot on top and the seam underneath.

Preheat a browning dish on high for five to seven minutes, or for the maximum time allowed in the manufacturer's instructions. Swirl the oil around the bottom of the dish and arrange the scrolls in the dish, seam side down and radiating outward like spokes of a wheel. Microwave on high for one minute; turn the scrolls over, using tongs, and cook for two minutes more on high, turning both the scrolls and the dish at least twice during this time. Allow to rest for 30 seconds, then cut one of the scrolls in half to check for doneness. If no pink meat is visible, the scrolls are done; otherwise, cook for another 30 seconds on high, rest the scrolls for a few seconds, and test again.

To make the glaze, combine the honey, lime or lemon juice, orange juice, balsamic vinegar, soy sauce, and thyme, and cook on high for three minutes. Remove the thyme sprigs. Stir the arrowroot into the glaze and cook on high for 45 seconds more, stirring

halfway through. Brush the scrolls with the glaze and serve at once.

SUGGESTED ACCOMPANIMENTS: *cooked carrots; potatoes.*

EDITOR'S NOTE: *For the mixed fresh herbs, use a selection of the following: tarragon, basil, marjoram, oregano, thyme, mint, and sage. If you wish, omit the glaze and season the scrolls simply with a little salt and some ground pepper.*

Stewed Fennel with Ham

Serves 4
Working time: about 5 minutes
Total time: about 20 minutes

Calories **130**
Protein **8g.**
Cholesterol **30mg.**
Total fat **10g.**
Saturated fat **4g.**
Sodium **315mg.**

4 oz. ham, trimmed of fat
8 small fennel bulbs (about 4 lb.)
1 tbsp. finely chopped fresh thyme, or 1 tsp. dried thyme leaves
½ cup white wine
4 tbsp. unsalted vegetable stock (recipe, page 139)
freshly ground black pepper
2 tbsp. unsalted butter (optional)

Cut a thin slice off the root of each fennel bulb and trim off the tops of the stems; reserve the feathery tops.

Put the fennel, thyme, white wine, stock, some pep-

per, and the butter, if you are using it, into a dish. Cover and microwave on high until the fennel is cooked through—about 15 minutes. Meanwhile, cut the ham into fine dice and add it to the dish one minute before the end of the cooking time. Garnish with the feathery tops of the fennel, torn into small pieces.

SUGGESTED ACCOMPANIMENTS: *plain boiled rice; green salad.*

EDITOR'S NOTE: *Belgian endive or onions can be substituted for fennel. Allow two whole vegetables per person and cook for only 10 minutes; garnish with chopped parsley.*

Grape Leaves Stuffed with Pork and Rice

Serves 4
Working (and total) time: about 25 minutes

Calories **220**
Protein **15g.**
Cholesterol **45mg.**
Total fat **12g.**
Saturated fat **4g.**
Sodium **250mg.**

½ lb. lean ground pork
12 large grape leaves
1 cup cooked brown rice
2 tsp. dried oregano
¼ tsp. salt
freshly ground black pepper
1 tbsp. fresh lemon juice
2 tbsp. virgin olive oil
1¼ cups unsalted chicken stock (recipe, page 139)
lemon slices for garnish (optional)

If you are using fresh grape leaves, put them into a bowl and cover generously with water. Microwave on high until boiling—about five minutes; set them aside for 10 minutes, then remove the leaves and trim away the stalks. If you are using grape leaves preserved in brine, blanch them in boiling water for two to three minutes to remove the salt, then rinse them well and remove the stalks.

Mix together the pork, rice, oregano, salt, and some pepper. Place a spoonful of the pork mixture in the center of each leaf, wrap over one end, then the two sides, and roll up into a neat parcel.

Pack the rolled grape leaves tightly in a single layer in a shallow casserole, with their seams underneath. Pour in the lemon juice, oil, and stock, which should almost cover the parcels. Cover the dish and microwave on medium for 10 minutes. Serve the grape leaves hot or cold; if you are serving them hot, the cooking liquid may be poured over them. Garnish with the lemon slices, if you are using them.

SUGGESTED ACCOMPANIMENTS: *Greek salad; crusty bread.*

Chicken Stock

Makes about 2 quarts
Working time: about 20 minutes
Total time: about 3 hours

4 to 5 lb. uncooked chicken trimmings and bones (preferably wings, necks, and backs), the bones cracked with a heavy knife
2 carrots, sliced into ½-inch rounds
2 celery stalks, sliced into 1-inch pieces
2 large onions (about 1 lb.), cut in half, one half stuck with 2 cloves
2 sprigs fresh thyme, or ½ tsp. dried thyme leaves
1 or 2 bay leaves
10 to 15 parsley stems
5 black peppercorns

Put the chicken trimmings and bones into a heavy stockpot and pour in enough water to cover them by about 2 inches. Bring the liquid to a boil over medium heat, skimming off the scum that rises to the surface. Boil the liquid gently for 10 minutes, skimming and adding a little cold water from time to time to help precipitate the scum.

Add the carrots, celery, onions, thyme, bay leaves, parsley, and peppercorns; submerge them in the liquid. If necessary, add enough additional water to cover the vegetables and bones. Reduce the heat to low and simmer the mixture for two to three hours, skimming as needed to remove the scum.

Strain the stock and allow it to stand until tepid, then refrigerate it overnight or freeze it long enough for the fat to congeal. Spoon off and discard the layer of fat.

Tightly covered and refrigerated, the stock may safely be kept for three to four days. Stored in small, tightly covered freezer containers and frozen, the stock may be kept for as long as six months.

EDITOR'S NOTE: *The chicken gizzard and heart may be added to the stock. Wings and necks—rich in gelatin—produce a particularly gelatinous stock, ideal for sauces and jellied dishes. The liver should never be used.*

Veal Stock

Makes about 3 quarts
Working time: about 30 minutes
Total time: about 4½ hours

3 lb. veal breast or shank meat, cut into 3-inch pieces
3 lb. veal bones (preferably knuckles), cracked
2 onions, quartered
2 celery stalks, sliced
1 carrot, sliced
8 black peppercorns
3 unpeeled garlic cloves (optional), crushed
1 tsp. fresh thyme, or ¼ tsp. dried thyme leaves
1 bay leaf

Fill a large pot halfway with water. Bring the water to a boil, add the veal meat and bones, and blanch them for two minutes to clean them. Drain the meat and bones in a colander, discarding the liquid. Rinse the meat and bones under cold running water and return them to the pot.

Add the onions, celery, carrot, peppercorns, and garlic, if you are using it. Pour in enough water to cover the contents of the pot by about 3 inches, and bring the water to a boil over medium heat. Lower the heat to maintain a simmer, and skim any impurities from the surface. Add the thyme and bay leaf, and simmer the stock very gently for four hours, skimming occasionally.

Strain the stock into a large bowl, then cool it as for chicken stock and spoon off the congealed fat.

EDITOR'S NOTE: *Any combination of veal meat and bones may be used to make this stock; ideally, the meat and bones together should weigh about six pounds. Ask your butcher to crack the bones.*

Vegetable Stock

Makes about 2 quarts
Working time: about 25 minutes
Total time: about 1 hour and 30 minutes

3 celery stalks with leaves, finely chopped
3 carrots, sliced into ⅛-inch-thick rounds
3 large onions (about 1½ lb.), coarsely chopped
2 large broccoli stems, coarsely chopped (optional)
1 medium turnip, peeled and cut into ½-inch cubes
5 garlic cloves, coarsely chopped
½ cup coarsely chopped parsley (with stems)
10 black peppercorns
2 sprigs fresh thyme, or 1 tsp. dried thyme leaves
2 bay leaves

Put the celery, carrots, onions, broccoli, if you are using it, turnip, garlic, parsley, and peppercorns into a heavy stockpot. Pour in enough water to cover them by about 2 inches. Slowly bring the liquid to a boil over medium heat, skimming off any scum that rises to the surface. When the liquid reaches a boil, add the thyme and bay leaves. Stir the stock once, reduce the heat to low, and let the stock simmer undisturbed for one hour.

Strain the stock into a large bowl, pressing down lightly on the vegetables to extract all their liquid. Discard the vegetables. Allow the stock to stand until it is tepid, then refrigerate or freeze it.

Tightly covered and refrigerated, the stock may safely be kept for five to six days. Stored in small, tightly covered freezer containers and frozen, the stock may be kept for as long as six months.

Glossary

Allspice: the dried berry of a member of the myrtle family. Used whole or ground, it is called allspice because its flavor resembles a combination of clove, cinnamon, and nutmeg.

Arrowroot: a tasteless, starchy, white powder refined from the root of a tropical plant; it is used to thicken purees and sauces. Unlike flour, it is transparent when cooked.

Arugula (also called rocket): a peppery-flavored salad plant with long, leafy stems, popular in Italy.

Balsamic vinegar: a mild, extremely fragrant wine-based vinegar made in northern Italy. Traditionally, the vinegar is aged for at least seven years in a series of casks made of various woods.

Basil: a leafy herb in the mint family with a strong, pungent aroma when fresh. Covered with olive oil and refrigerated in a tightly sealed container, fresh basil leaves may be kept for several months.

Baste: to help brown and flavor a food, and keep it from drying out, by pouring pan drippings or other liquid over it during cooking.

Bay leaves: the aromatic leaves of *Laurus nobilis*—a Mediterranean evergreen—used fresh or dried to flavor stocks and stews. When dried bay leaves are broken, they have very sharp edges and can cause internal injuries, so they should be removed before serving.

Blanch: to partially cook food by briefly immersing it in boiling water. Blanching makes thin-skinned fruits and vegetables easier to peel; it can also mellow strong flavors.

Bouquet garni: several herbs—the classic three are parsley, thyme, and bay leaf—tied together or wrapped in cheesecloth and used to flavor a stock or stew. The bouquet garni is removed and discarded at the end of the cooking time.

Brown cap mushrooms (also called chestnut mushrooms): a brown-skinned variety of mushroom with a firm texture and a strong flavor.

Bulb fennel: see Fennel.

Bulgur: whole wheat kernels that have been steamed, dried, and cracked.

Calorie (or kilocalorie): a precise measure of the energy food supplies when it is broken down for use in the body.

Cardamom: the bittersweet, aromatic dried seeds or whole pods of a plant in the ginger family. Cardamom seeds may be used whole or ground.

Caul: a weblike fatty membrane that lines a pig's intestines. When wrapped around a lean ground-meat filling, it melts during cooking and moistens the meat.

Cayenne pepper: a fiery powder ground from the seeds and pods of red peppers; used in small amounts to heighten other flavors.

Chervil: a lacy, slightly anise-flavored herb often used as a companion to other herbs, such as tarragon and chives. Because long cooking may kill its flavor, chervil should should not be added until the last minute.

Chili peppers: hot or mild red, yellow, or green members of the pepper family. Fresh or dried, most chili peppers contain volatile oils that can irritate the skin and eyes; they must be handled carefully (*see caution, page 36*).

Cholesterol: a waxlike substance that is manufactured in the human body and also found in foods of animal origin. Although a certain amount of cholesterol is necessary for proper body functioning, an excess can accumulate in the arteries, contributing to heart disease. See also Monounsaturated fat; Polyunsaturated fat; Saturated fat.

Cilantro (also called fresh coriander or Chinese parsley): the pungent, peppery leaves of the coriander plant or its earthy-tasting dried seeds. It is a common seasoning in Middle Eastern, Oriental, and Latin American cooking.

Coulis: a sieved vegetable or fruit puree.

Couscous: a fine-grained semolina pasta; it is served with the classic North African stew of the same name.

Crème fraîche: a slightly ripened, sharp-tasting French cream.

Cumin: a slightly bitter spice used in curry and chili powders.

Daikon radish: a long, white Japanese radish.

Dark sesame oil: a dark seasoning oil made from toasted sesame seeds, high in polyunsaturated fats, with a nutty, smoky aroma. Because the oil has a relatively low smoking point, it is rarely heated.

Dates: the fruit of the date palm, dates can be bought fresh or dried. When dried dates are specified, choose plump unpitted dates in preference to pressed slab dates.

Deglaze: to dissolve the browned bits left in a pan after roasting or sautéing by stirring in wine, stock, water, or cream.

Degrease: to remove the accumulated fat from stock or cooking liquid by skimming it off with a spoon or blotting it up with paper towels. To eliminate the last traces of fat, draw an ice cube through the warm liquid; the fat will cling to the cube.

Dietary fiber: a plant-cell material that passes undigested through the human body but promotes healthy digestion of other food matter. The fiber in this book is provided mainly by fresh and dried fruit and by certain vegetables such as peas and beans.

Dijon mustard: a smooth or grainy hot mustard once manufactured only in Dijon, France; it may be flavored with herbs, green peppercorns, or wine.

Fava beans (also called broad beans): a European variety of bean, eaten fresh or dried. The thick pods and thin skins must be removed from all but the youngest fava beans.

Fennel: (also called Florence fennel or *finocchio):* a vegetable with feathery green tops and a thick, bulbous stalk. It has a milky, licorice flavor and can be eaten raw or cooked. The tops are used both as a garnish and as a flavoring. Fennel is sometimes incorrectly labeled as anise.

Fennel seeds: the aromatic dried seeds from herb fennel, a relative of vegetable fennel; used as a licorice-flavored seasoning in many Italian dishes. Fennel is also used in curries and to make five-spice powder.

Fiber: see Dietary fiber.

Fines herbes: a mixture of finely chopped fresh herbs that incorporates parsley plus one or more other herbs, such as chives, tarragon, and chervil.

Five-spice powder: a pungent blend of ground Sichuan pepper, star anise, cassia, cloves, and fennel seeds; available in Asian food markets.

Fructose: a sugar found in honey and many fruits, fructose is the sweetest of all natural sugars. It can be bought as a powder and looks much like ordinary sugar. Since a smaller amount of fructose is needed, the calorie count is reduced.

Ginger: the spicy, buff-colored rhizome, or rootlike stem, of the ginger plant, used as a seasoning either in fresh form or dried and powdered. Dried ginger makes a poor substitute for fresh ginger.

Harissa: a fiery-hot North African condiment, based on cayenne pepper.

Hoisin sauce: a thick, dark, reddish brown soybean-based Chinese condiment.

Hot red-pepper sauce: a hot, unsweetened chili sauce, such as Tabasco® or the Thai siracha sauce.

Julienne: to slice food into matchstick-size pieces.

Juniper berries: the dried berries of the juniper tree, used as the key flavoring in gin. They lend a resinous tang to marinades and sauces.

Kohlrabi: a cruciferous vegetable with an enlarged stem in the form of a light green or lavender bulb.

Kumquat: a small, bittersweet citrus fruit resembling a tiny orange.

Lemon grass (citronella): a long, woody, lemon-flavored stalk that is shaped like a scallion. Lemon grass is available in Asian food markets.

Lemon verbena: a lemon-flavored herb native to South America and widely cultivated in Europe, available as fresh or dried leaves. In dried form, it is often used to make herbal tea.

Mace: the ground aril, or covering, that encases the nutmeg seed.

Mango: a fruit grown throughout the tropics, with sweet, succulent, yellow-orange flesh that is extremely rich in vitamin A. It may cause an allergic reaction in some individuals.

Medallion: in pork cooking, a round or oval-shaped slice of lean pork, for frying, grilling, or broiling.

Mixed spices: a mixture of spices and herbs, including several of the following: nutmeg, mace, cinnamon, cayenne pepper, white pepper, cloves, ground bay leaf, thyme, marjoram, and savory.

Monounsaturated fat: one of the three types of fats found in foods. Monounsaturated fats are believed not to raise the level of cholesterol in the blood.

Nappa cabbage (also called Chinese cabbage): an elongated cabbage that resembles romaine lettuce, with long, broad ribs and crinkled, light green leaves.

Nonreactive pan: a cooking vessel whose surface does not chemically react with food. This includes stainless steel, enamel, glass, and some alloys.

Okra: the green pods of a plant indigenous to Africa, where it is called gumbo. In stews, okra is prized for its thickening properties.

Passion fruit: a juicy, fragrant, egg-shaped tropical fruit with wrinkled skin, yellow flesh, and many small black seeds. The seeds of the passion fruit are edible; the skin is not.

Phyllo: a Greek pastry dough that is rolled and stretched to tissue-paper thinness. Phyllo is often available frozen.

Pine nuts (also called *pignoli):* seeds from the cones of the stone pine, a tree that is native to the Mediterranean. Toasting brings out their buttery flavor.

Polyunsaturated fat: one of the three types of fats found in foods. They exist in abundance in such vegetable oils as safflower, sunflower, corn, and soybean. Polyunsaturated fats lower the level of cholesterol in the blood.

Porcini (also called *cepes):* wild mushrooms with a pungent, earthy flavor that survives drying or long cooking. Dried porcini should be soaked in water before they are used.

Prosciutto: an uncooked, dry-cured, and slightly salty Italian ham, sliced paper thin.

Pureed tomatoes: a puree made from peeled fresh or canned tomatoes. Available commercially, but it should not be confused with the thicker, concentrated tomato paste sometimes labeled tomato puree.

Recommended Dietary Allowance (RDA): the average required daily amount of an essential nutrient as determined for groups of healthy people of various ages by the National Research Council.

Reduce: to boil down a liquid in order to concentrate its flavor and thicken its consistency.

Retsina: a Greek wine flavored with pine resin.

Rice-paper wrappers: brittle wrappers for spring rolls made from rice flour, available in stores specializing in Southeast Asian foods. They are softened by dipping them in water.

Ricotta: a soft, mild, white Italian cheese, made from cow's or sheep's milk.

Saffron: the dried yellowish red stigmas (or threads) of the crocus, which yield a pungent flavor and a bright yellow color. Powdered saffron is less flavorful than the threads.

Salsify (also called oyster plant): a slender, tapering root, about twice the length of a carrot, with a white or yellowish skin and a faint oysterish flavor.

Saturated fat: one of the three types of fats found in foods. They exist in abundance in animal products and coconut and palm oils; they raise the level of cholesterol in the blood. Because high

blood-cholesterol levels may contribute to heart disease, saturated fat consumption should be restricted to less than 15 percent of the calories provided by the daily diet.

Sausage casings: natural casings, stronger than commercial casings, are the cleaned intestines of lamb, pig, or ox. Usually sold preserved in brine or dry salt, they can be ordered from butchers or specialty suppliers and should be soaked before use. Lamb casings are generally used for thin sausages; pig or ox casings for thicker ones.

Sear: to brown the surface of meat by a short application of intense heat; searing adds flavor and color, but it does not seal in meat juices.

Sesame oil: see Dark sesame oil.

Sherry vinegar: a full-bodied vinegar made from sherry; its distinguishing feature is a sweet aftertaste.

Shiitake mushroom: a variety of mushroom, originally grown only in Japan, sold fresh or dried. The dried form should be soaked and stemmed before use.

Sichuan pepper (also called Chinese pepper, Japanese pepper, or anise pepper): a dried shrub berry with a tart, aromatic flavor that is less piquant than black pepper.

Sodium: a nutrient essential to maintaining the proper balance of fluids in the body. In most diets, a major source of the element is table salt, which contains 40 percent sodium. Excess sodium may contribute to high blood pressure, which increases the risk of heart disease. One teaspoon of salt, with 2,132 milligrams of sodium, contains about two-thirds of the maximum "safe and adequate" daily sodium intake recommended by the National Research Council.

Soy sauce: a savory, salty brown liquid made from fermented soybeans and available in both light and dark versions. One tablespoon of regular soy sauce contains 1,030 milligrams of sodium; lower-sodium variations used in the recipes in this book may contain half that amount.

Star anise: a woody, star-shaped spice, similar in flavor to anise. Ground star anise is a component of five-spice powder.

Stir-fry: to cook cubes or strips of meat or vegetables, or a combination of both, over high heat in a small amount of oil, stirring constantly to ensure even cooking in a short time. The traditional cooking vessel is a Chinese wok; a heavy-bottomed

frying pan may also be used for stir-frying.

Sun-dried tomatoes: tomatoes that have been dried in the open air to concentrate their flavor; some are then packed in oil. Most sun-dried tomatoes are of Italian origin.

Sweet potato: either of two types of a nutritious tuber grown in the United States. One type has yellowish, mealy flesh; the other has moist, sweet, orange flesh and is often sold as a yam. Both varieties differ from the African yam that is sold in some ethnic markets, and both are unrelated to white potatoes.

Tamarind concentrate: the brown, acidic-flavored pulp from the seed pod of the tamarind tree, available in Asian food markets.

Tenderloin (also called fillet): the most tender muscle in the pig's carcass, located inside the loin.

Tomato paste: a concentrated tomato puree, available in cans and tubes, used in sauces and soups. See also Pureed tomatoes.

Total fat: an individual's daily intake of polyunsaturated, monounsaturated, and saturated fats. Nutritionists recommend that total fat constitute no more than 30 percent of the energy in the diet. The term as used in this book refers to the combined fats in a given dish or food.

Turmeric: a yellow spice used as a coloring agent and occasionally as a substitute for saffron. It has a musty odor and a slightly bitter flavor.

Walnut oil: an oil extracted from pressed walnuts. It should be purchased in small quantities; once opened, it can turn rancid within a few weeks.

Water chestnut: the walnut-sized tuber of an aquatic Asian plant, with rough brown skin and white, sweet, crisp flesh. Fresh water chestnuts may be refrigerated for up to two weeks; they must be peeled before use. To store canned water chestnuts, first blanch or rinse them, then refrigerate for up to three weeks in fresh water changed daily. Jerusalem artichoke makes an acceptable substitute.

White pepper: a powder ground from the same dried berry as that used to make black pepper, but with the berry's outer shell removed before grinding, resulting in a milder flavor. White pepper is used as a less visible alternative to black pepper in light-colored foods.

Wild rice: the seeds of a water grass native to the Great Lakes region of the United States. Wild rice is appreciated for its robust flavor.

Index

Picture Credits

Credits from left to right are separated by semicolons, from top to bottom by dashes.

Cover: Martin Brigdale. 4: Chris Knaggs—John Elliott (2). 5: Jan Baldwin—John Elliott; Chris Knaggs. 6: Martin Brigdale. 11-16: John Elliott. 17, 18: Jan Baldwin. 19: James Murphy. 20: John Elliott. 21: Chris Knaggs. 22: John Elliott. 23: Chris Knaggs. 24: John Elliott. 25: Chris Knaggs. 26, 27: James Murphy. 28: John Elliott. 29: John Elliott (3)—Philip Modica. 30: Chris Knaggs. 31: John Elliott. 32, 33: Chris Knaggs. 34: James Murphy. 35: Philip Modica. 36: John Elliott. 37: Chris Knaggs. 38: Jan Baldwin. 39-41: Chris Knaggs. 42, 43: Jan Baldwin. 44, 45: John Elliott. 46: James Murphy. 47: Chris Knaggs—John Elliott (3). 48, 49: James Murphy. 50: Chris Knaggs. 51: Jan Baldwin. 52: James Murphy. 53: Jan Baldwin. 54: Philip Modica. 55: Chris Knaggs. 56: James Murphy. 57: Philip Modica. 58: Jan Baldwin. 59: Chris Knaggs. 60: James Murphy. 61, 62: John Elliott. 63: James Murphy. 64, 65: John Elliott. 66, 67: Philip Modica. 68: Chris Knaggs. 69, 70: John Elliott. 71: Jan Baldwin. 72: Philip Modica. 73: Chris Knaggs. 74: John Elliott. 75: James Murphy. 76: John Elliott. 77: Chris Knaggs. 78: Jan Baldwin. 79: Philip Modica. 80: John Elliott. 81: Philip Modica. 82: James Murphy. 83: James Murphy—Chris Knaggs. 84: Philip Modica. 85: James Murphy. 86: Jan Baldwin. 87: James Murphy. 88: John Elliott. 89: James Murphy. 90: John Elliott. 91: James Murphy. 92, 93: Chris Knaggs. 94, 95: Philip Modica. 96, 97: James Murphy. 98, 99: John Elliott. 100, 101: Jan Baldwin. 102: John Elliott. 103-105: James Murphy. 106: Chris Knaggs. 107: James Murphy. 108: Jan Baldwin. 109: Philip Modica. 110, 111: James Murphy. 112: Chris Knaggs. 113: Jan Baldwin. 114: Philip Modica. 115: James Murphy. 116, 117: John Elliott. 118: Philip Modica. 119: John Elliott. 120: Chris Knaggs. 121, 122: Philip Modica. 123: James Murphy. 124: Chris Knaggs. 126: James Murphy. 127-129: Chris Knaggs. 130, 131: James Murphy. 132, 133: Chris Knaggs. 134: John Elliott. 135: Chris Knaggs. 136, 137: James Murphy. 138: Chris Knaggs.

Props: The editors wish to thank the following outlets and manufacturers; all are based in London unless otherwise stated. Cover: china, Villeroy & Boch; cloth, Osborne & Little plc; flatware, Mappin & Webb Silversmiths. 5: *(top)* platter, Villeroy & Boch; knife, Mappin & Webb Silversmiths. 16: plates, Royal Worcester, Worcester. 17: marble, W. E. Grant & Co. (Marble) Ltd. 19: plate, Royal Worcester, Worcester. 21: platter, Villeroy & Boch. 22: plate, Royal Worcester, Worcester. 26: plate, Villeroy & Boch. 30: plates, Hutschenreuther (U.K.) Ltd. 36: plate, Royal Worcester, Worcester. 37: plate, Rosenthal (London) Ltd. 38: bowl, Birgit Blitz, Gruiten, Germany. 40: bowl *(bottom, left)*, Arthur Griffiths, The Craftsmen Potters Shop. 42: plate, Line of Scandinavia. 43: plate, Tony Gant, The Craftsmen Potters Shop. 46: bowls, David Mellor. 48, 49: marble, W. E. Grant & Co. (Marble) Ltd. 50: plate, Rosenthal (London) Ltd.; flatware, Mappin & Webb Silversmiths. 52: plate, Villeroy & Boch; cloth, Osborne & Little plc. 53: plate, Hutschenreuther (U.K.) Ltd.; flatware and napkin ring, Mappin & Webb Silversmiths; candlestick, Royal Copenhagen Porcelain and Georg Jensen Silversmiths Ltd. 54: bowl, David Mellor; fabric, Osborne & Little plc. 55: plate and vegetable dish, Rosenthal (London) Ltd. 58: platter, Spode, Worcester. 59: plate, Fortnum & Mason; flatware and wine-bottle coaster, Mappin & Webb Silversmiths. 61: Formica, Newcastle, Tyne and Wear. 62: china, Royal Copenhagen Porcelain and Georg Jensen Silversmiths Ltd.; flatware, Mappin & Webb Silversmiths. 69: plate, Rosenthal (London) Ltd. 70: plate, Royal Worcester, Worcester. 71: plate, Hutschenreuther (U.K.) Ltd.; peppermill, Royal Copenhagen Porcelain and Georg Jensen Silversmiths Ltd. 72: plate, Rosenthal (London) Ltd.; flatware, Mappin & Webb Silversmiths. 73: plate, Royal Worcester, Worcester. 74: bowl, David Mellor; napkin, Ewart Liddell. 77: bowl, Mary Rose Hudson. 78: dish, Jenny Clarke, The Craftsmen Potters Shop; marble, W. E. Grant & Co. (Marble) Ltd. 79: bowls, Winchcombe Pottery, The Craftsmen Potters Shop. 80: dish and plate, Wedgwood. 81: plate, Rosenthal (London) Ltd.; flatware, Next Interiors. 84: flatware, Mappin & Webb Silversmiths. 87: platter, Hutschenreuther (U.K.) Ltd.; flatware, Mappin & Webb Silversmiths. 88: plate, Tony Gant, The Craftsmen Potters Shop. 89: fork, Next Interiors. 90: napkin, Ewart Liddell. 92, 93: plate, Jane Hamlyn, The Craftsmen Potters Shop; marble, W. E. Grant & Co. (Marble) Ltd. 94: bowl, Mid Wales Development Centre; marble, W. E. Grant & Co. (Marble) Ltd. 98, 99: marble, W. E. Grant & Co. (Marble) Ltd. 100: casserole, David Mellor. 101: platter, Villeroy & Boch; knife, Mappin & Webb Silversmiths. 102: plate, Rosenthal (London) Ltd. 104: plate, Villeroy & Boch; napkin, Ewart Liddell. 105: plate and dish, Winchcombe Pottery, The Craftsmen Potters Shop. 106: plate, Thomas (London) Ltd. 108: plate, Line of Scandinavia. 109: plate, Thomas (London) Ltd. 111: rug, Kilkenny; flatware, Fortnum & Mason; bowl, Tony Gant, The Craftsmen Potters Shop. 112: napkins, Kilkenny. 113: plate, Inshop. 115: plate, Hutschenreuther (U.K.) Ltd.; flatware, Mappin & Webb Silversmiths. 118: plate, Fortnum & Mason; Formica, Newcastle, Tyne and Wear. 119: marble, W. E. Grant & Co. (Marble) Ltd. 120: platter, Rosenthal (London) Ltd. 122: marble, W. E. Grant & Co. (Marble) Ltd. 124: dish, Arthur Griffiths, The Craftsmen Potters Shop. 126: plate, Villeroy & Boch. 128: platter, Rosenthal (London) Ltd. 132: place mat, Ewart Liddell. 136: plate, Villeroy & Boch.

Acknowledgments

The index for this book was prepared by Myra Clark, London. The editors also wish to thank the following: Rachel Andrew, London; Steve Ashton, London; J. Blackburn, Devon; René Bloom, London; Nora Carey, Hartford, Connecticut; Sean Davis, London; Jonathan Driver, London; Elizabeth David Ltd., London; Richard Guy, Wiltshire; Molly Hodgson, Yorkshire; Isabella Kranshaw, London; Brian Leonard, London; Christine Noble, London; Philomena O'Neill, London; Perstorp Warerite Ltd., London; Katherine Reeve, London; Yens Roesner, London; Sharp Electronics (U.K.) Ltd., London; Jane Stevenson, London; Dr. T. Stuttaford, London; Toshiba (U.K.) Ltd., London; Paul van Biene, London.

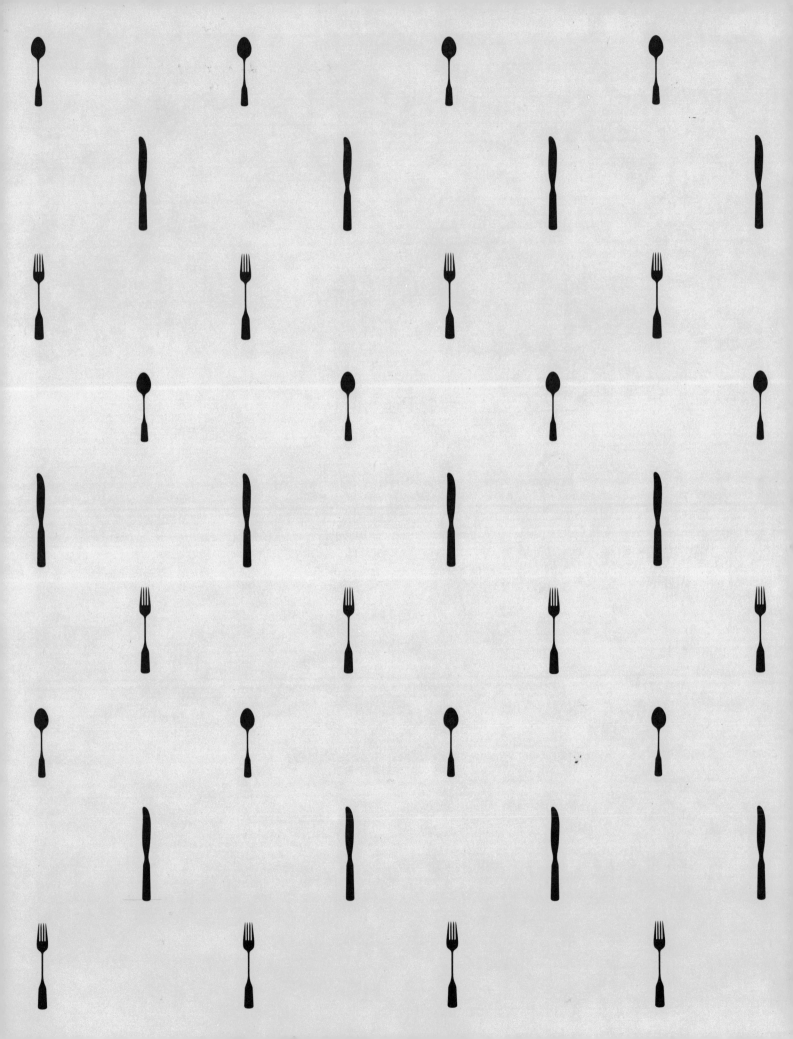